Developing Democratic Education

edited by
Clive Harber

Education Now Books

Published 1995 by Education Now Publishing Co-operative
P.O.Box 186, Ticknall, Derby

Copyright © 1995 Education Now Publishing Co-operative

British Library Cataloguing in Publication Data

Developing Democratic Education
    I. Harber, Clive
    370.115

ISBN   1-871526-22-1

Design and production: Education Now Books

Cover design: James Meighan

Printed by Mastaprint, Sandiacre, Nottinghamshire

Contents

Education Now is a forum in which people with differing, diverse and undogmatic views can develop ideas about constructive alternatives to the existing regressive forms of education, through open debate and publishing.

Introduction

In January 1995, the first international audit of children's rights in Britain accused government ministers of repeatedly violating the UN convention on the rights of the child which it had signed up to four years previously. One criticism was that children are not consulted over the running of their school and should be taught about their rights in school.

This book stems, therefore, from what was a very timely one day conference on democratic education organised by the Education Now research, writing and publishing co-operative and held at Bilston Community College, Wolverhampton in October 1994. The keynote address did in fact outline the increasing international salience of the debates about democratic education and was itself very critical of Britain in this regard. This address forms Chapter 1 of the book and the eleven further chapters are based on workshops held at the conference that covered a variety of themes related to democratic education. Some of these chapters are written to reflect what actually happened in the workshop on the day while others summarise debates, evidence and experience relevant to the theme of the workshop.

The result is a volume which explores both the management and curriculum of democratic education and which, while not ignoring theory, is also firmly grounded in the practice of democracy in educational institutions and the realities of the contexts in which they operate.

Clive Harber
University of Birmingham and University of Natal, South Africa.

Democratic Education and the International Agenda

by Clive Harber

Introduction

Two thousand five hundred years ago the Greek philosopher Aristotle wrote in his book *The Politics*,

> *"But of all the safeguards that we hear spoken of as helping to maintain constitutional continuity the most important, but most neglected today, is education, that is educating citizens for the way of living that belongs to the constitution in each case. It is useless to have the most beneficial rules of society fully agreed on by all who are members of the polity if individuals are not going to be trained and have their habits formed for that polity, that is to live democratically if the laws of the society are democratic and oligarchically if they are oligarchic" (1962:215/6).*

This chapter will argue that there is now an emerging international consensus that democracy is the preferred form of government and that democratic education is necessary to help to sustain democracy in the longer term. In so doing it will cover a number of key themes in the debates about democratic education. These are as follows:

- What evidence is there that education for democracy is now high on the international agenda and why?
- Why is education as currently structured predominantly authoritarian?
- What sort of democracy is it that we should be educating for?
- What is a democratic school and why is a democratic school more effective?
- What examples of good practice and educational democratisation are there internationally?

Democracy and the International Agenda

In the last four or five years there has emerged a growing international consensus on the need for democratic government. The West has long favoured democracy for itself but it has been equivocal and contradictory about supporting it in other contexts, particularly in developing countries. However, even a brief perusal of the documentation on what is termed 'good government' produced by, for example, the two key aid bodies in Britain, the ODA and the British Council, makes it very clear that the good government they are promoting around the rest of the world is essentially democratic government. They are not alone in this. The writer has recently examined the policy statements of the government aid agencies of the USA, Canada, Finland, Norway and Denmark and they are all now in agreement on this. Even the United Nations after many years of sitting on the fence now makes very clear statements to the effect that political freedom and democracy are an essential ingredient of human development. The UNDP human development report, for example, says:

> *"The purpose of human development is to increase people's range of choices. If they are not free to make those choices, the entire process becomes a mockery. So, freedom is more than an idealistic goal - it is a vital component of human development. People who are politically free can take part in planning and decision-making. And they can ensure that society is organised through consensus and consultation rather than dictated by an autocratic elite" (1992:26).*

This new international consensus that good government equals democratic government is the result of a number of factors. First and foremost has been the collapse of communism and the conversion of the one party state in eastern Europe to the multi-party state. The major political alternative to democracy now no longer exists and therefore also no longer provides a model for developing countries to follow. Thus the most recently independent states in Africa, for example, - Eritrea, Namibia and South Africa - have all followed a democratic route. Moreover, in order to encourage democracy, international agencies increasingly attach political strings to loans and aid - no democracy, no money. A second factor has been that it is patently clear that authoritarian regimes whether in eastern Europe, Latin America, Asia or Africa have not worked in that they have been no more successful at providing economic growth and social welfare than democratic regimes. Thus the argument that it is necessary to suspend democracy and human rights in order to achieve economic and social development is no longer credible. Indeed, a recent article in *The Economist* magazine argued strongly that on the whole the evidence suggests that democracy actually improves economic performance, noting that:

"The claim that authoritarian government works best for development is a claim about history - but it draws mainly on evidence from one region East Asia, over a comparatively short period. The evidence is anyway unpersuasive: East Asia may well be special, but not because it has had authoritarian rulers" (August 27 - September 2 1994).

Indeed, if authoritarian governments were the key to economic success then Africa would be an economic giant which it clearly is not.

It also has to be noted that the discipline of political science is not entirely blameless in this regard. When modern political scientists first became interested in issues of political development in the early 1960s, they clearly saw some form of democracy as the goal of political development. By the mid to late 1960s, however, with America increasingly involved in counter insurgency abroad and civil unrest over the Vietnam war at home, this emphasis changed from democracy to regimes that could provide stability and order. Political 'modernisation' as it was termed was seen in technocratic and bureaucratic terms of efficient government - issues of freedom and human rights were secondary (Higgott 1983). Very recently, however, this has come full circle and there is a renewed interest in the whole field of democracy and democratic political culture in relation to developing countries (Diamond 1993).

If there is now a new consensus on the need for democratic government then what is the role of education in helping to make democracy sustainable in the longer term? This role has recently been described very succinctly by the British Overseas Development Administration,

"The relationship between education and the political process is highlighted in the recent ODA Technical Note on Good Government. The relationship is illustrated in Eastern Europe and the former Soviet Union, where the process of democratisation is seen to be hampered by curricula based on authoritarian philosophies and characterised by rote learning. Citizens who have been exposed to learning styles which require the questioning of assumptions, empirical styles of study and the exploration of alternatives are seen as likely to have more chance of participating fruitfully in a pluralistic political process than those who have not" (ODA,1994:3).

It is also interesting that to the knowledge of the writer, in the last two years there have been conferences on the theme of education and democracy in

Jerusalem, Israel; Washington, U.S.A.; Copenhagen, Denmark; Tromso, Norway; Cape Town, South Africa and at least three in Britain. Indeed, the Adam Institute for Democracy and Peace, which organised the Jerusalem conference, is now attempting to establish an International Centre for Education for Democracy in a Multicultural society. The good news is that education for democracy is suddenly high on the international agenda. The bad news is that internationally education is presently still predominantly authoritarian.

Schools as Authoritarian

Bowles and Gintis in their book *Schooling in Capitalist America* ask 'Why in a democratic society should an individual's first real contact with a formal institution be so profoundly anti-democratic?' (1976:250-1).   A nation-wide survey in the United States demonstrated that schooling occurs almost entirely in a teacher-directed manner. The author says,

> *"Somewhere, I suspect down in the elementary school, probably in the fifth and sixth grades, a subtle shift occurs. The curriculum subjects, topics, textbooks, workbooks and the rest - comes between the teacher and the student. Young humans come to be viewed only as students, valued primarily for their academic aptitude and industry rather than as individual persons preoccupied with the physical, social and personal needs unique to their circumstances and stage in life."*
> *(Goodlad,1984:80)*

Further north, in Canada, Michael Fullan and his colleagues used 3,600 questionnaires in a survey of students in Ontario schools. They found that:
* only a minority of students think that teachers understand their point of view and the proportion decreases with educational level
* less than one fifth of the students reported that teachers asked for their opinions and ideas in deciding what or how to teach
* principals and vice principals were not seen as listening to, or being influenced by students
* substantial percentages of students, including one out of every two high school students, reported that 'most of my classes are boring' (Fullan,1991:171).

In Britain schools are also authoritarian organisations. The final paragraph in Stephen Ball's study of the micro politics of British schools, for example, reads as follows,

"beyond the attempt at theorising school organisation, another fundamental question is begged. Is the organisational life presented here the only possible form of running schools? The answer must be 'no', and as I see it the alternative lies in the direction of school democracy." *(1987:280)*

Charles Handy, who is a professor of business organisation, studied British secondary schools and compared their organisational style to prisons in that the inmates' routine is disrupted every 40 minutes, they change their place of work and supervisors constantly, they have no place to call their own and they are often forbidden to communicate with each other. In another way, he suggested, schools are like factories and the pupils like products which are inspected at the end of the production line, sometimes rejected as sub-standard and then stamped 'English', 'history', 'maths' etc. Handy's survey also asked the teachers in the schools how many people there were in the organisation and they answered 10 or 70 or whatever - they nearly always left out the pupils (Handy 1984).

The situation in Britian has been made worse by the introduction in 1988 of a centralised, bureaucratised and prescriptive national curriculum. Not only does this leave little room for pupil or teacher choice in terms of the content of learning but its emphasis on 'facts' rather than skills or values has meant a push back towards rote, retention and regurgitation. Moreover, it is a complete negation of the idea of education for democracy as it deliberately excludes, as will be argued in more detail later on, any attempt to educate directly and systematically about contemporary society by excluding all reference to the social sciences such as politics, sociology and economics.

The picture in developing countries is also bleak in terms of education for democracy. School classrooms in Africa, for example, have been described by one African sociologist as follows,

"In most African schools the classroom is highly structured in terms of the formal distribution of space. The teacher in the classroom exercises unquestioned authority in such matters as seating arrangements and movement. He or she not only initiates the activities to be pursued by

pupils, but also controls communication channels and all types of interaction within the group. We do not know the extent to which this kind of classroom environment determines the political orientation of pupils but enforced conformity to an authority system throughout early childhood and early adolescence if supplemented by other factors is likely to encourage passive acceptance of authority in later years. A democratic and participatory classroom, on the other hand, is supposed to contribute to the development of a critical and reflective attitude among pupils" (Datta,1984:40).

However, in Chinese countries the situation seems little different. One study put it that,

"The teacher as high authority figure seems pan-Chinese, a fact verified by the dominance of the lecture method and teacher-centred classrooms not only in Taiwan but also in the People's Republic and Hong Kong" (Meyer,1988:34).

Finally, a recent survey in fourteen countries in South and Central America found that whereas teachers claimed to use a variety of teaching methods such as role play, debate, conferences, lectures, guest speakers and field trips, the pupils responded that they experienced only listening to the teacher, memorising, writing down and coping (Villegas-Reimers, 1993). It also ought to be noted that the evidence is that classroom practices in countries that have termed themselves socialist such as Tanzania and Cuba are no different (Bowles 1976; Mbilinyi 1979).

Why is this the case? Why are schools and classrooms organised in an authoritarian manner that gives little real power to pupils? There are several possible explanations. The first is historical. Modern mass schooling has its origins at the end of the nineteenth century when the predominant mode of manufacturing and commercial organisation was large scale bureaucracy. Thus schools for the mass of ordinary children were organised along bureaucratic lines. Marten Shipman in his book *Education and Modernisation* captures this nicely when he says that,

"Punctuality, quiet orderly work in groups, response to orders, bells and timetables, respect for authority, even tolerance of monotony, boredom, punishment, lack of reward and regular attendance at place of work are the habits to be learned at school" (1971:54/5).

Schools, therefore, were organised along bureaucratic-authoritarian lines essentially as a preparatory socialisation for subordinate jobs in factories and offices. This model of schooling was then imposed through colonialism in other parts of the world and has been perpetuated in the post-colonial era because it has suited the interests of post-colonial governments. This is Bruce Fuller writing on Malawi but making a wider point:

"The younger, more fragile state, common across the Third World, plays a much stronger role in importing and legitimating the bureaucratic structure and moral order of the Western school. Bureaucratic administration signals "modern practice", particularly in societies where rationalised organisations or firms are still a novel form. Here the visible contours and symbols of "modern organisation" take on enormous power. The Third World school may fail to hold deep effects on children's acquired literacy or secular values. But the fact that the school is tightly administered - with tidy accounts, a sharp schedule of classes and attractive gardens - signals the attributes of a modern organisation. The institution is recognised by local parents as a concrete instrument of modernity, even if the school's technical objective of raising literacy is rarely accomplished" (1991:43/4).

Concomitant with this style of school organisation was a view of knowledge as scientific and objective, of their being one true answer to questions, even if that answer had not yet been found. Schools, therefore, were about the transmission of true facts to young minds. This view of the nature of knowledge has obvious implications for both school and classroom organisation - if education is a body of facts to be learned there is little need for discussion or investigation. Moreover, the school is thus divided into hierarchies of those who 'know' (the teachers) and those who do not (the pupils).

This form of school organisation for the mass of children who pass out to take up subordinate jobs (or to have no job at all) also, of course, suits those with political power. It is an education in domination and submission not one of enquiry and independent critical thought. This, presumably, is why most governments around the world have not been in any hurry fundamentally to alter the nature of schooling. Few governments want a politically informed, articulate, confident and critical population - and I am referring here to many governments in democracies as well as in authoritarian regimes.

Britain's record on educating its citizens for democracy is particularly deficient with nothing in the curriculum even approximating to the sort of political education required in a mature, modern democracy. But then that is probably because Britain with its Monarchy, its aristocratic upper chamber - the House of Lords, its lack of freedom of information, its unwritten constitution and absence of a Bill of Rights, its unrepresentative electoral system and its increasing rule by unelected NGOs is not a mature and modern democracy anyway. A recent opinion survey for Channel 4's *Bite the Ballot* season of television programmes on democracy found that 30% - that is almost a third - of the sample thought that Britain was not a democratic country. Only 21% agreed that there was nothing wrong with the system of government - four fifths thought there was something wrong *(The Observer 1/5/94)*. The result of this lack of emphasis on democracy and education for democracy, unfortunately, is that survey after survey shows that young people in Britain are not only politically ignorant but also a disturbingly high proportion hold openly racist values which is hardly compatible with a healthy, multi-cultural democracy. They themselves say that this is by default - if they had had political education at school this would not necessarily be the case (McGurk,1987:51; Banks et al 1992:187). As Adolf Hitler said, *'What good fortune for those in power that people do not think'*.

The Aims of Democratic Education

What sort of democracy should we be educating for? Obviously the formal structures of democracy include mechanisms of representative and accountable government which protects human rights and the rule of law. This includes, for example, a choice of political parties, the freedom to organise into pressure groups and a free and diverse mass media. In terms of education this implies both a certain minimum level of political knowledge of the the political system and political issues and the development of political skills such as detecting bias, arguing a case and participating in group decision making.

There is, however, a second aspect of democracy at the level of civil society and that is the need to create what Almond and Verba (1963) once termed as a 'civic culture', that is a political culture not only supportive of democracy at the macro level but which also supports and encourages democracy at the level of everyday life in the workplace, in leisure organisations and in the home. An interesting example of this comes from America where a group called the Centre for Living Democracy promotes the idea that the way to combat the feelings of powerlessness and apathy that have become widespread in America is not to leave everything to the government but to realise that the 'solutions to today's problems require the ingenuity and commitment of people most directly affected' and that it is important that ordinary citizens discover that they have a vital role in solving public problems. They argue that democracy is in itself a rewarding way of life that involves schools, workplaces, community initiatives, media, government, religious groups and human services. They say,

> *"Citizens of a Living Democracy are not born. We learn the arts of democracy - just as we learn sports, history or reading. We learn by experience and by training."*

They go on to list some of these arts of democracy which include

- *Dialogue - which is not the same as debate but is public talk in which participants learn as well as teach*
- *Negotiation - which involves moving beyond pre-set positions to solve problems by identifying shared interests*
- *Political Imagination - which means letting go of today's "givens" in order to re-image the future*
- *Public Judgement - which is richer than simple opinion and derives from dialogue and reflection*
- *Evaluation and Reflection - which means continually incorporating the lessons our experiences offer*
(Centre for Living Democracy, Undated).

As these arts of democracy suggest, democracy is not just about participating, it is also about **how** we participate. Participation rates were high in Nazi Germany and the Soviet Union but this did not make them into democracies. There are important procedural values underlying democracy both at the macro, formal level and at the micro level of everyday life. These include, for example, tolerance of diversity and mutual respect between individuals and groups, a respect for evidence in forming opinions, a willingness to be open to the possibility of changing one's mind in the light of such evidence, the possession of a critical stance towards political information and regarding all people as having equal social and political rights as human beings. In other words there is, or should be in a democracy, an emphasis on reason, open-mindedness and fairness. These are the some of the values that education for democracy must foster, for as the Schools Council in Britain put it,

"Some values, like those of democracy, tolerance and responsibility, grow only with experience of them. Social education arises from a school's ethos, its organisation and its relation with the community. The way a school organises its staff and pupils and its formal rules, says a great deal about its real values and attitudes. Schools need to practise what they seek to promote" (1981).

The Nature of Democratic Schooling

What is a democratic school? Is it more effective than a conventional authoritarian school and why? While the workings of individual democratic primary and secondary schools in various countries in Europe, North America and Africa have been described in a number of sources (Greenberg 1985; Gordon 1986; Harber 1993; Harber and Meighan 1989; Jensen and Walker 1989), there is no single, clearcut organisational model of a democratic school or college and perhaps by definition if people are deciding for themselves on the shape of the organisation there ought not to be. Any such school must involve a shift of power and authority away from staff to students, both in terms of decisions about how the institution as a whole is run, and in terms of what is learned in the classroom and how. In terms of the whole school or college, this usually means some sort of elected council which represents staff, students and parents and perhaps some significant others such as community leaders or, in the UK context, school governors. The powers of such a council will vary according to the age of the pupils but must include matters which are of significance to them. As one sixth former at a British school put it:

"Half-hearted attempts at pupil involvement are worse than useless, a smokescreen which is easily seen through. Most sixth formers will recognise the sixth form committee which is patronised, kept away from significant issues and limited to planning social events or the provision of snack dispensers" (The Guardian 17/7/90).

At Countesthorpe School in Leicestershire in Britain, which is a school for 14-18 year olds and which operated democratically from the early 1970s to the mid/late 1980s, the pupils were influential in decisions on abandoning school uniforms, the funding of a school minibus, smoking policy, the structure of the school day, music in the school and student-teacher ratios (Gordon,1986:Chapter 12).

In terms of curriculum and classroom method, the democratic school or college is one where students have some say both over what is learned and how. The students can have some real power over curriculum because there is some genuine choice involved, whether this be in terms of subject options or topics to be studied individually or in groups within subjects. Teaching and learning in such a situation will be characterised by a variety of teaching methods but will regularly include those such as discussions and projects where the students themselves are influential in shaping the direction the work takes.

Obviously there is a long continuum of possible levels of choice and freedom for students in terms of curriculum, from complete freedom such as exists at Summerhill School in the UK and Sudbury Valley school in America to situations where, despite a national curriculum, schools manage to build in some subject options and allow some self-direction in coursework. Paradoxically, however, complete freedom is not necessarily democratic. Most societies are confronted with serious forms of inequality and prejudice - in Britain and in America, for example, racism is a major problem - in African societies ethnicity is a major issue. If schools do nothing to counter the racism or ethnic prejudice that exists in the surrounding society then they are guilty of reproducing it by default. Therefore a democratic school that does not expose its pupils to anti-racist and anti-sexist education is not democratic because racism and sexism are themselves anti-democratic in that they do not regard people as being equal and having the same rights simply because they are human. A democratic school, therefore, must be involved in the promotion of equal opportunities at some point in the curriculum and in whole school policies.

Why is such a democratic school a more effective school and what evidence is there that supports this contention? The reasons why democratic schools are more effective are quite simple.

- First, rules are better kept by staff and students if democratically agreed to in the first place.
- Second, communications in the school or college are improved.
- Third, there is an increased sense of responsibility as staff and students have more control over their own organisation.
- Fourth, decision-making is improved as a range of internal and external interests and opinions is considered.

Studies of school effectiveness have in fact found that effective school management is related to staff having a sense of control over the school programme, and worthwhile and efficient inter-departmental meetings and planning exercises. This sense of involvement and influence in the institution is also true of students. A favourable school climate has been linked with students sensing that the school as a social system is not a meaningless environment in which they can exert little control over what happens to them (Reid, Holly and Hopkins,1987). Michael Rutter and his associates in their book *15,000 Hours* found that schools that give a large proportion of students responsibility had better exam results, better behaviour and attendance and less deliquency. Trafford's recent case study of the democratisation of Wolverhampton Grammar School in Britain, interestingly called *Sharing Power in Schools: Raising Standards (1993)*, and his subsequent research on the school both suggest that there has been an improvement in examination results since the process of democratisation began. In Africa where schools are often plagued by conditions of financial stringency and poor resourcing there is evidence that student involvement in school management can help enhance school effectiveness - or perhaps more realistically reduce ineffectiveness (Harber 1993). A longtitudinal study of the graduates of Sudbury Valley School in America looked at effectiveness in a rather different manner. It examined what had happened to a sample of 76 students after they had left school and concluded that not only had they not suffered as a result of attending such a school but had gone on to good colleges and got good jobs because the school had created traits in them such as a strong sense of responsibility, the ability to take the initiative and solve problems, an ability to communicate effectively and a high commitment to the field in which employment is sought (Gray and Chanoff, 1986).

Of course, it is only possible to measure effectiveness in terms of some sort of outcomes or goals - effectiveness at achieving what? Conventional studies of school effectiveness use more easily quantifiable indicators such as examination performance and truancy rates but a democratic school would also have as its aim the creation of citizens more capable of participating in a democratic manner. Research findings from America, Britain and Tanzania all suggest that such schools had contributed to the development of both participatory skills and the values of operating democratically (Hepburn 1984, John and Osborne 1992, Harber 1993). Moreover, there is also evidence that more open, democratic classrooms making greater use of discussion and other participatory methods can foster a range of democratic political orientations such as greater political interest, less authoritarianism, greater political knowledge and a greater sense of political efficacy (Ehman,1980). Significantly, democratic and co-operative teaching methods have also been shown to reduce inter-ethnic conflict and promote cross-cultural friendship (Lynch, 1992:22). A recent study of five 'racially' mixed schools in the south eastern United States compared two more participant schools that stressed co-operative learning, the development of interpersonal relationships, values clarification and the heterogeneous grouping of students with three other more traditional schools where students were streamed by achievment and taught in lecture-recitation style in predominantly same-'race' classes. The study found that cross-'race' interaction and friendships and a positive evaluation of different 'race' students were significantly higher in the more participant schools than the more traditional, authoritarian ones (Conway and Damico, 1993).

A good deal of evidence therefore suggests that democratic schools are more effective schools and the present authoritarian structure of most schools is ineffective. Handy and Aitken in their book *Understanding Schools as Organisations* say,

> *"Interestingly, however, modern businesses are moving away from hierarchies towards networks in response to the need for more flexibility and in order to give more room to the individual. It may be that in aping the bureaucracy of large businesses the secondary school has been adopting a theory of management that is already out of date" (1986:95).*

International Case Studies of Educational Democratisation

Finally, it is instructive to look briefly at some examples of efforts towards educational democratisation from around the globe to see that the sort of arguments and evidence outlined above are being taken very seriously in some quarters. In America, for example, the Institute for Democracy in Education is an organisation which believes that restructuring for democratic education must come at the heart of education. It provides a network for teachers, parents, students and administrators who are committed to education for democracy through conferences and the production of a journal. It is based at the University of Ohio but has 24 offices in the USA and Canada and now a branch has been opened in Britain at the University of Birmingham.

A recent book on effective schools in developing countries (Levin and Lockheed 1993) looked at a number of case studies of projects which had been designed to enhance school effectiveness in conditions of financial stringency, low levels of completion and low levels of achievment. It found a number of common themes. The following were two of them,

> *"Empowerment. A principal emphasis is placed on empowering teachers, students, parents and the community to take responsibility for making educational decisions and for the consequences of those decisions. At the heart of the educational philosophy is the view that meaningful education requires active participation among all those who are involved in the process rather than following a script or formula set out by higher levels."*

> *"Active Learning. The emphasis on student learning is to shift from a more traditional passive approach in which all knowledge is imparted from teachers and textbooks to an active approach in which the student is responsible for learning. Effective school approaches emphasise self instruction ... problem solving and meaningful applications." (15/16)*

One of the case studies discussed in the book by Levin and Lockheed is the New School Programme in Colombia, South America. This is a programme which is aimed at improving primary schools in rural areas, was designed and tested during a fourteen year period, implemented in 17,000 schools and reached more than 900,000 children. In terms of curriculum the New School Programme promotes active and reflective learning, the ability to think, analyse, investigate, create, apply knowledge and improve children's self esteem. It seeks to develop children's co-operation and solidarity and to promote civic, participatory and democratic attitudes. In terms of school government, the school is seen as an organisation where children can be introduced to a civic and democratic way of life. Children are organised into committees where they learn group decision making responsibilities and co-operative attitudes (Colbert, Chiappe and Arboleda, 1993).

An interesting example of a country where an attempt is being made to democratise the whole education system is Namibia. Until 1990 Namibia was known as South West Africa and was governed by South Africa under its apartheid policies. Since independence the SWAPO government has not only set about ensuring greater access to education for black students but has also introduced a new philosophy of what it terms 'learner-centred education'. The following comes from a recent book published for the Ministry of Education in Namibia called *Toward Education for All* (1993) and which has a supporting foreword from both the President, Sam Nujoma, and the Minister of Education, Nahas Angula:

"To develop education for democracy we must develop democratic education...Our learners must study how democratic societies operate and the obligations and rights of their citizens. Our learners must understand that democracy means more than voting ... (and) ... that they cannot simply receive democracy from those who rule their society. Instead, they must build, nurture and protect it. And they must learn that they can never take it for granted. In the past we were fooled by an authoritarian government that preached to us about democracy. Nor will learners today be deceived by an education system that talks about democracy and says it is for someone else at some other time. To teach about democracy our teachers and our education system as a whole must practice democracy." (41)

A major thrust of the argument for democratising education in Namibia has been that in the new context of education for all, teacher-centred education is ineffective:

"As we make the transition from educating an elite to education for all we are also making another shift, from teacher-centred to learner-centred education. That change, too, will seem troubling at first and will take us some time to accomplish successfully. We are accustomed to classrooms where attention and activities are focused on the teacher. Indeed, we have probably all encountered teachers set in their ways that pay little attention to the backgrounds, interests and orientations of their students...Few people learn easily or well in that setting. Much of the significant learning that does take place is accomplished despite, not because of, the teacher. Teacher-centred instruction is inefficient and frustrating to most learners and certainly is inconsistent with education for all" (10).

As this quotation suggests, the Ministry is very well aware of the obstacles to learner-centred education and has, for example, launched new programmes of initial and in-service teacher education based on democratic and participatory principles and is in the process of reforming the assessment system in order to make it much less based on memorisation, much more skills based and much more diverse in the assessment techniques used.

Conclusion

For Namibia, then, as increasingly for other countries, good government can only take place within a democratic framework and education must help to sustain this democratic framework. The bottom line importance of education for democracy is dramatically underlined in the following change of mind described by Stephen Heyneman, an education official at the World Bank in Washington:

> *"Wherever I have worked over the last decade I have recommended the use of educational vouchers and other measures to maximise user choice. But after working on the educational problems of Central and Eastern Europe and the Russian Federation, I have changed my opinion. My view has changed not because educational efficiency is no longer important. Rather, it has changed because I have discovered that the importance of educational efficiency has a limit. In the case of Russia, I have been working in an ethnically heterogeneous, federal system, much like our own, but falling apart. More than 100 ethnic groups now may control schools and, not having the traditional restraints, may now be able - if they choose - to teach disrespect for the rights of their neighbours. Schools can contribute to armageddon, and I have been forced to learn that there are things in life - such as civil unrest and civil war - which are more expensive and important that an inefficient and cumbersome public education system. But let me begin at the beginning. What is there that makes an education system essential for a consensus of democratic values and for the creation of a democratic society?"* (Heyneman 1995:1).

This is a question that this book and many in education are now beginning to address.

References

Almond, G. and Verba, S. (1963) *The Civic Culture* Princeton: Princeton University Press.

Aristotle (1962) *The Politics* Harmondsworth: Penguin.

Ball, S. (1987) *The Micro-Politics of the School* London: Methuen.

Banks, M. et al (1992) *Careers and Identities* Milton Keynes: Open
    University Press.

Bowles, S. (1976) 'Cuban education and revolutionary ideology' in
    P. and G. Figueroa (Eds.) *Sociology of Education: a Caribbean
    Reader* Oxford: Oxford University Press.

Bowles, S. and Gintis, H. (1976) *Schooling in Capitalist America* New York:
    Basic Books.

Centre for Living Democracy (Undated) *Democracy Is Not What We Have
    ...Democracy Is What We Do* Battleboro.

Conway, M. and Damico, S. (1993) 'Facing up to Multiculturalism: Means as
    Ends in Democratic Education', paper delivered to the International
    Conference on Education for Democracy in a Multicultural Society,
    Jerusalem, Israel.

Colbert, V., Chiappe, C. and Arboleda, J. (1993) 'The New School Program:
    More and Better primary Education for Children in Rural Areas in
    Columbia' in H.Levin and M.Lockheed (Eds.) *Effective Schools in
    Developing Countries* London: Falmer Press.

Datta, A. (1984) *Education and Society: A Sociology of African Education*
    London: MacMillan.

Diamond, L. (Ed.) (1993) *Political Culture and Democracy in Developing
    Countries* Boulder: Lynne Rienner.

Ehman, L. (1980) 'The American High School in the Political Socialisation
    Process' *Review of Educational Research*, 50.

Gray, P. and Chanoff, D. (1986) 'Democratic Schooling: What Happens to
    Young   People Who Have Charge of Their Own Education?',
    American Journal of Education 94, 2.

Fullan, M. (1991) *The New Meaning of Educational Change* London:
    Cassell.

Fuller, B. (1991) *Growing Up Modern* London: Routledge.

Gordon, T. (1986) *Democracy in One School* Lewes: Falmer Press

Goodlad, J. (1984) *A Place Called School* New York: McGraw-Hill.

Greenberg, D. (1985) *The Sudbury Valley School Experience* Framingham: The Sudbury Valley School Press.

Handy, C. (1984) *Taken For Granted? Looking at Schools as Organisations* York: Longmans.

Handy, C. and Aitken, R. (1986) *Understanding Schools as Organisations* Harmondsworth: Penguin.

Harber, C. and Meighan, R. (1989) *The Democratic School: Educational Management and the Practice of Democracy* Ticknall: Education Now.

Harber, C. (1993) 'Democratic Management and School Effectiveness in Africa: Learning from Tanzania', *Compare* 23,3.

Hepburn, M. (1984) 'Democratic Schooling - Five Perspectives from Research', *International Journal of Political Education*, 6

Heyneman, S. (1995) 'Good Educational Governance:An American Export', *The American School Board Journal* (Forthcoming)

Higgott, R. (1983) *Political Development Theory* London: Croom Helm.

Jensen, K.and Walker, S. (1989) *Towards Democratic Schooling: European Experiences* Milton Keynes: Open University Press.

John, P. and Osborn, A. (1992) 'The Influence of School Ethos on Pupils' Citizenship Attitudes', *Educational Review* 44, 2.

Levin, H. and Lockheed, M. (Eds.) (1993) *Effective Schools in Developing Countries* London: The Falmer Press.

Lynch, J. (1992) *Education for Citizenship in a Multicultural Society* London: Cassell.

Mbilinyi, M. (1979) 'Secondary Education' in H.Hinzen and V.Hundsdorfer (Eds.) *The Tanzanian Experience* London: Evans.

McGurk, H. (1987) *What Next?* London: Economic and Social Research Council.

Meyer, J. (1988) 'Moral Education in Taiwan', *Comparative Education Review* 32.

Namibia Ministry of Education and Culture (1993) *Toward Education For All* Windhoek: Gamsberg MacMillan.

Overseas Development Administration (1994) *Aid to Education in 1993 and Beyond* London: ODA.

Reid, K., Hopkins, D., and Holly, P. (1987) *Towards the Effective School* Oxford: Blackwell.

Rutter, M.,Maughan, B., Mortimore, P., and Ouston, J. (1979) *Fifteen Thousand Hours* London: Open Books.

Schools Council (1981) *The Practical Curriculum* London: Methuen.

Shipman, M. (1971) Education and Modernisation London: Faber.

Trafford, B. (1993) *Sharing Power in Schools: Raising Standards* Ticknall: Education Now.

U.N.D.P. (1992) *Human Development Report* New York: UNDP

Villegas-Reimers, E. (1993) 'Where Do We Go From Here?' *Colloquium On Education For Democracy:Proceedings of a Workshop* Washington: USAID.

Democratic Primary Education

by Clive Harber

Introduction

A major theme underlying this book, and one which is articulated in the opening chapter, is that a more democratic school is a better school. If this is generally the case, is it true at all levels of schooling? This section of the book discusses this and related questions at a series of educational levels. It is important, however, to begin with primary schools as the one objection often raised is that pupils of primary school age are too young and immature to participate and that therefore mistakes and wrong decisions would be made.

Age and Democratic Education

The argument that pupils of primary school age are too young to be involved in democratic participation at school misses the key point that the reason for involvement is the importance of beginning to learn democratic values and skills through experience. If this 'too young' argument were, for example, to be applied to the learning of language or walking, then nobody would be allowed to talk or walk until full mastery of the language and perfect balance had been attained. In learning, getting it wrong is part of getting it right.

In fact, political socialisation research has shown that children begin to develop political values and attitudes as young as three or four years old (Stacey 1978) while research on the political cognitive development of children (Connel 1971, Stevens 1982) suggests that even during primary school children have the necessary conceptual equipment to understand the main political ideas involved. What they lack is the necessary knowledge, skills, values and experience and this is what participation helps to teach them. The problem, therefore, is not whether primary school children can be involved in democratic participation as age is not necessarily a barrier. The question is rather how to best to organise their involvement so that their democratic skills will develop with increasing maturity.

Two Case Studies

This section of the chapter describes two primary schools which have operated in a democratic manner in order to provide an immediate 'feel' of what a democratic primary school might look like. The following section will then discuss the effectiveness of democratic primary education.

The first example comes from The Netherlands. In a primary school in a small town near to Amsterdam in 1980, a school parliament was established which met every month and which formed an integrated part of the decision-making structure of the school. Each class elected two representatives and then briefed them on the subjects they wanted to have debated when the parliament met - questions as to whether the school should start earlier and finish earlier, what the playing fields should be used for and whether and on which days animals should be allowed into the classroom (highly contentious). Almost the entire functioning of the school parliament depended on the children themselves. At the start the headteacher chaired the meetings but this function was taken over by one of the children elected by other members and, apart from the minute-taker, the only other adult present was a member of the 'ouderraad' - a sort of parent-teacher association. After each monthly session the minutes were written up, copied and distributed to each class which discussed them on the following school day - making sure to question their representative on the extent to which he or she had carried out their wishes.

In an interview published in the Dutch newspaper *de Volkskrant*, the headteacher explained that it was the policy of the school to adopt rules only after full discussion by the children, but he also found that the parliament system which they had adopted was quickly teaching the children some important lessons. Thus, not only did each class follow the debates of the parliament in which its motions were discussed, but the children also learned to select their representatives with care, giving preference to those who would express their viewpoint adequately rather than to someone who is popular. In addition the headteacher found that the children were much more willing voluntarily to abide by rules which they had some part in making than by any rules 'handed down' (Cohen 1981).

In the early 1980s Rosendale Junior School in South London also introduced a system whereby each term every class elected representatives to a school council after nominations, hustings and a secret ballot. The council met weekly during lesson times for about 50 minutes and was chaired by a teacher. The representatives then went back to their classes with the minutes and themselves chaired meetings at which council decisions were discussed and further issues raised. In the older classes particularly, teachers took a back seat and they too had to raise their hands if they wanted to speak.

The council even had its own budget. In 1983 the council decided to spend £120 of profits from the school calendar and tuck shop (itself established by the school council) on the purchase of balls, cricket bats and skipping ropes for the playground and an aquarium for the library. Examples of other decisions taken by the school council included:

- teachers should not jump the queue for dinners
- toilet doors should be higher and locks repaired
- a table-tennis and CB radio club should be established
- Friday afternoon assemblies should begin earlier
- more advanced reading books should be purchased
- the tuck shop should be opened two playtimes a week, drinks should be sold (but not sweets) and each child should be allowed to spend a maximum of 20p. (Agreed after parental opinion was tested with a questionnaire.)
- uniform should not be introduced
- pork and beef sausages should not be mixed up at lunchtime because of the eating rules of the different religions

Teachers at the school saw the council as an education in democracy. Children learn the language and practice of democratic politics - meeting, discussion, chair, election, vote, candidate, minutes, majority, representative and debate. The head retained the right of veto and complaints against individual teachers were out of order. If an idea was impractical then the head had to explain why this was so. He attended one meeting, for example, to explain why, for safety reasons, certain playground areas were out of bounds, but he never had to issue a blunt 'no' (*Sunday Times* 8/5/83).

Primary School Councils and Enhanced Effectiveness

One recent study of 123 primary schools in Canada found that where schools had councils (56 of the 123) they were in practice only given a very limited role confined to fund raising and planning social events. Yet in the two schools where genuine provision was made for student council input on school issues staff and pupils alike agreed that the pupil council input was invaluable in the solution of school problems. The authors commented that:

"The failure of administrators and teachers to give students more opportunities for input into the running of schools represents a great loss to education. Numerous studies have pointed to the substantial benefits that accrue to both students and schools when there are effectively functioning student councils in schools. What is perhaps even more important is that students' basic attitudes towards politics are shaped by students' participation in school governance" (Robinson and Koehn 1994: 26).

One example of a project that has been recently researched is the Pupils Councils Programme in Liverpool (Khaleel 1993). This is a project which exists in five inner city schools. Such schools are often marked by unacceptably high levels of bullying, truancy, confrontation and teacher stress. The project therefore aims to create an environment where anti-social behaviour is recognised as being unacceptable by giving pupils a sense of their own ability to do something to change the climate of opinion in the school. The main mechanism for this is the establishment of representative school councils of which two are in primary schools.

At one of the two primary schools, for example, the council has dealt with such issues as:
- fixing holes in the playground
- children going to the shops without permission
- keeping the playground clean
- getting permission before going after balls that go over the fence
- using a lighter ball for football to stop windows getting broken
- keeping parked cars in one corner of the playground

Councillors have also received suggestions from pupils who wanted a fancy dress party, to restart country dancing and have a disco more often.

Through dealing with such issues, which are of considerable importance to pupils of this age themselves, school councils can provide a valuable introduction to democratic practice which is relevant to their level of education. While the councils had only been in operation for two years when the evaluative research was undertaken, it was clear that both schools had taken on the issues of bullying, fighting and vandalism with some success. Indeed, the study expressed its main conclusions in terms of three programme objectives that were considered to be good indicators of progress and which would be easy to measure in all five schools, including the primary schools. These were as follows:

> *1. "'To develop the realisation by pupils that they have a positive role to play in creating a caring community within the school'. On this the research concluded that it had been shown that as a result of the Pupil Councils Programme almost all the pupils interviewed, and indeed other pupils who have been involved in the programme within the five schools, do now realise that they have a positive role to play in creating a caring school community. This is because the ideas and issues they have brought up regarding aspects of school life have been discussed, tackled and implemented with relative success."*

> *2. "'To improve relationships between teachers and pupils inside and outside the classroom'. The research report showed that as a result of the Pupil Councils Programme there has been a marked improvement in the relationships between teachers and pupils in all of the five schools, in particular with the pupil councillors. Teachers commented that they now have a democratic relationship with pupils rather than the traditional authoritarian/passive relationship."*

> *3. "'To increase involvement in pupil initiated extra curricular activities'. The report shows that as a result of the Pupil Councils Programme there has been a significant increase in the involvement of pupil-initiated extra curricular activities in all of the five schools. Pupils are now coming forward with their ideas to improve all aspects of school life, from a litter patrol to improve the school environment, to ideas to improve educational and leisure activities, to posters to combat bullying and vandalism." (Khaleel 1993).*

Conclusion

Political values and attitudes start to form from a very early age and it is important that these develop in a democratic direction. Primary schools can provide a valuable introduction to democratic practice which is relevant to the age of the pupils. When such an introduction is provided, they seem to take it on in a mature and sensible manner, and this improves school climate and management.

References

Cohen, L. (1981) 'Political literacy and the primary school: a Dutch experiment', *Teaching Politics* 10,3.

Connel, R. (1971) *The Child's Construction of Politics* Melbourne: University of Melbourne Press.

Khaleel, M. (1993) *Pupil Councils First Independent Monitoring Programme* Liverpool: Girobank.

Robinson, N. and Koehn, D. (1994) 'Student councils in primary schools: contributors to management decisions?' *Management in Education* 8,1.

Stacey, B. (1978) *Political Socialisation in Western Society* London: Edward Arnold.

Stevens, O. (1982) *Children Talking Politics* Oxford: Martin Robertson.

Democratising Secondary Schools

by Derry Hannam

Introduction

The workshop was attended by a stimulatingly diverse group of educational academics, practitioners at various levels, and administrators from schools systems from four continents. Despite the diversity, ground rules were quickly established.

It was agreed not to spend too long considering the philosophical aspects of democracy. A working definition of "the acquisition of a voice by and the sharing of power amongst the stakeholders in a community/organisation/group" was accepted along the lines developed in Pateman (1970), with an emphasis on direct participation and not just representation. The various stakeholders with a direct interest in a secondary school were listed. These included taxpayers through central or local government, parents, the local community, local employers, governing bodies or their equivalent, teachers and other school staff and of course the pupils/students.

There was strongly-felt support for the view set out in Fullan (1982 and 1991) that most pupils/students in most schools in most countries, including avowed democracies, were subjected to experiences that were predominantly profoundly undemocratic. It was unanimously felt that Fullan was correct in thinking that little had changed in the decade between the two editions of his book in that schools "...rarely think of students as participants in a process of change and organisational life..." and that benefits would flow "...if we treated the student as someone whose opinion mattered..." (Fullan 1991, p170). The work of Handy (1984) was also quoted in support as was the keynote paper for this conference (Harber, introduction to this volume). Thus participants established the position that whilst the participation of all stakeholders was the ideal for a school to be democratic their wish was to focus on the most commonly and most inappropriately unvoiced and disempowered group - the pupils/students. Participants from several countries noted that although there was talk of "empowerment" in curriculum discussion there was little sign of students/pupils having or sharing any actual power in their schools.

Democratic Practice

Perhaps because of the predominance of practitioners in the workshop it was decided to assume that the participation of pupils/students in democratic decision making was a good thing and ought to be happening. The urgent need was felt to be for practical guidance as to how to make it happen rather than to seek to justify that it should happen - "We know it works. Why doesn't it happen? How can we make it happen?"

It was felt that although it should in theory be easier to democratise a secondary than a primary school as the pupils/students were older and hopefully more mature, nonetheless their organisational complexity made the task in many ways more difficult. In fact the founder of the charity Schools Councils UK, Teddy Gold, was a participant and was able to describe some outstandingly successful (though also, sadly, outstandingly rare) examples of highly pupil participative primary schools on Merseyside that are being supported by SCUK. Smallness, the continuity of teacher/pupil relationship, and the opportunity for intensive and direct involvement by the headteachers were felt to be significant factors in their success. These headteachers have expressed their great regret that the level of democratic opportunity that their pupils have become accustomed to managing with confidence by the time they leave, is not built upon by the neighbourhood secondary schools to which the pupils transfer. It was agreed that the capacities of younger children are routinely underestimated by secondary schools, doubtless contributing to the well researched (e.g. Hannam, 1993, or Keys and Fernandes, 1993) decline in pupil enthusiasm observed in Years 8 and 9 (12-14 year-olds). Secondary schools in all the countries represented in the workshop, with the exception of Denmark, tended to fragment learning group identity and teacher-pupil/student relationship from the end of the admission year if not before. In England and Wales the National Curriculum has increased this tendency to fragmentation of pupil experience due to the move away from integrated humanities and arts courses. This makes it difficult for any one group of pupils/students to have enough time together with any one teacher, or a small team of teachers, for direct democracy to function or for representation to be effective. That is unless the school is small by secondary school standards and can meet as a whole community. Examples such as Hadera in Israel, Sudbury Valley High in the USA or the private sector Sands School in Devon were mentioned. An alternative possibility might be substantially autonomous mini-schools into which a large secondary school can be broken down as advocated in Meighan and Toogood (1992), though hard to find in reality; or the school-within-a-school of the Kohlbergian Just

Community School model such as those at Scarsdale or Brookline Schools (Power, 1988) or Ted Sizer's Coalition of Essential Schools (Sizer, 1986) in the U.S.A. It was encouraging to see the UK NAPCE (National Association for Pastoral Care in Education) arguing strongly for just such a reorganisation/restructuring of secondary schools in their response to National Curriculum review proposals (NAPCE, 1993).

Emerging themes

The facilitator outlined the fields/headings which were emerging from his current research into examples of democratic practice and experimentation in secondary schools across Europe (including Russia), the U.S.A., Colombia, Australia and Israel. These included:-

• Political/Citizenship Education; a field perceptively reviewed from an Australian perspective by Gilbert (1994) and from a multi-cultural and global perspective by Lynch (1992) though set back in England and Wales by the Dearing National Curriculum Review (Dearing 1994) after initial encouragement as a National Curriculum Cross-Curricular Theme and the setting up of the Young Citizens Award Scheme. School Councils are often justified in this context and although in too many cases in England and Wales they make few significant decisions and have little real grass-roots pupil/student participation or involvement (Fogelman 1991) examples do exist where this is not the case. In fact in the "moral malaise" post-Bulger environment in the U.K. even junior education ministers argued that "...pupils themselves should help to draw up school rules..." though these ideas showed no sign of leaking into policy-making. (Eric Forth reported in *The Guardian* *9.12.93*).

• Environmental and Community Education; there are interesting examples of pupil/student participative projects in several countries such as those sponsored by Learning Through Landscapes in the UK (Lucas, 1994), again set back by the Dearing review. Linked to this are developments in Community Education projects in several countries, such as the Community Action by Schools Award in the UK and some of the work of Tony Gibson's UK Neighbourhood Initiative Foundation, which have involved secondary school pupils/students in both influencing and making key decisions. Research in this area is being done by Birte Ravn of the Royal Danish School for Educational Studies in Copenhagen. Communitarianism and its guru, Amitai Etzioni, supposedly an active influence on Tony Blair and the 'modernisers' in the UK

Labour Party, strongly advocates the restructuring of schools in the USA to place the emphasis on self-discipline, self-motivation and responsibility. (Etzioni, 1983).

● Moral education; where the work of Kohlberg in particular has generated democratic experimentation in the USA (Zalaznick 1980, Kohlberg 1985, Power 1985), Germany (Oser 1992), Switzerland and Israel, in the belief that moral learning takes place most effectively in the context of practical decision making in the administration of a 'Just Community'. Even the current Ofsted Framework of Inspection in England (OFSTED, 1994) is placing a new emphasis on the appreciation of the importance of pupils/students exercising responsibility in schools in the context of inspecting moral education and some of its documentation is emphasising the contribution that an effective school council can make to a school. There is a significant number of cases in the U.K. where schools are including pupils/students in their processes for dealing with bullying through courts, counselling. or conciliation.

● School Effectiveness/School Improvement; somewhat in the margins of studies in the UK such as Rutter et. al. (1979) and Mortimore et.al. (1988) and more centrally emphasised in the work of Wilson and Corcoran (1988) in the U.S.A. are to be found correlations between pupil/student involvement in responsibility sharing and school effectiveness as measured by conventional examination/test, truancy and drop-out indicators. As a consequence advocacy for the fuller participation of pupils/students in decision making is to be found in some School Improvement work such as the School Development Planning proposals of Hargreaves and Hopkins (1991), Leask (in Wallace (Ed) 1992), or Westminster City Council (O'Connor, 1994) in the U.K., the Blueprint 2000 (Florida Education Department, 1992), or the Escuela Nuova programme in Colombia (Colbert et.al in Levin and Lockheed (Eds) 1993). Studies of the effectiveness of radical experiments in giving pupils/students a very substantial say in the content of their curriculum, both in terms of content and learning style, are rare largely because the practice is rare - outside Denmark at least. One classic longitudinal study is that of more than sixty students of Sudbury Valley High School (Gray and Channoff, 1986).

● Human/Children's Rights; neglected or even regarded with hostility by the Department for Education and the teacher unions in England and Wales, though not by the Department of Health which supports the Children's Rights Development Unit. It framed the 1989 Children Act taking on board much of the thinking behind the UN Convention on the Rights of the Child (1990)

Article 12 of which stresses the right to consultation and participation "...in all matters affecting the child." Its only impact on English schools, however, is in the area of statemented special needs or disability in the Education Act of 1993, and the pastoral care side of residential schools (Morgan, 1993). Some other countries take Childrens' Rights more seriously in official education policy making. In Danish Folkeskole "...the choice of content and method is statutorily to be made jointly by teacher and pupils." (Undervisnings Ministeriet, 1994). In Russia "...the class collective (is) to be the important environment, condition and tool...for the exercise of rights and freedoms..." (Rogacheva, 1994) and the ex-Minister for Education, Dneprov, stresses the importance of children's rights in his 'Pedagogy of Cooperation' (Eklov and Dneprov, 1993).

● Education for a Democratic Workplace; there are the first signs that the emphasis on improved communication, devolution of and participation in decision making, flattening of hierarchies and sharing of power generally, to be found in much modern management theory and in the practice of some of the most successful innovative companies worldwide, is beginning to acquire a school dimension. The management gurus such as Tom Peters in the USA, John Harvey-Jones in the UK (*Times Educational Supplement* 8.7.94), Ricardo Semler (Caulkin, 1993; Semler 1992) in Brazil, are beginning to talk about the need to restructure secondary schools. "...it is secondary education where things go wrong. I think our secondary system needs a revolution." (Harvey-Jones, 1994). The spread of 'social ownership' in the USA now includes companies of the size of Trans World Airlines, the growth of quite advanced forms of Employee Share Ownership Programs (ESOPS) in the USA and Europe, the 'L'economie sociale' concept growing in the European Union despite government hostility in the UK which can be seen at work in the highly successful John Lewis Partnership - all these developments have implications for the creation of democratic/ participative approaches to pre-vocational education in secondary schools. As yet there is little evidence of this connection being made by education policy makers or school managements - though at the European Union level the recently retired Commissioner for Education, Training and Research, Antonio Ruberti, had certainly seen the link between education and the need for works councils identified in the Social Chapter of the Maastricht Treaty (Corbett, 1994). Some evidence of a new awareness in this area by Business Studies and Information Technology teachers had been observed by at least one Ofsted Inspector in a handful of UK comprehensive schools over the last twelve months.

The workshop debate

The workshop explored in a preliminary way the individual concerns of its participants, all of which connected with the introductory themes, which were of course themselves interconnected.

The urgent need to develop a sense of identity and ownership of their lives in inner city young people in the face of the collapse of social institutions and the crisis of law and order was set out. Evidence from Schools Councils UK that the systematic creation of school councils with real power and the strong support of senior managements could be successful was offered. This was encouraging in the face of current pressures for simplistic authoritarian 'remedies' from the right in the UK.

Strong interest was expressed in the connections between secondary school democracy and workplace democracy. None of the participants knew of any studies in this area and all agreed that research needed to be done.

The potential contribution to school democratisation of the arts area of curriculum experience was examined and the views expressed endorsed earlier research conducted by the facilitator (Hannam, 1992).

The rest of the all too limited workshop time was spent exploring issues of power and how to bring about change in personal attitudes, institutions and cultures where authoritarian traditions supported existing vested interests. How to ensure that pupil power does not limit itself just to a selected or even elected elite but truly involves all pupils/students. How to convince the sceptical teacher, headteacher, administrator or politician that the perceived risks involved in sharing power are worth taking. That the loss of one kind of status and security can be replaced by more creative alternatives. That the risks of not changing are greater than the risks of change. How to prevent new cohorts of teachers, especially those entering schools with a wish to work democratically (if they belong to the small minority who have experienced such approaches in their training), from succumbing to authoritarian pressures once immersed in an authoritarian school culture. How to attract into teaching people who do not have psychological needs to control others. How to dare to make a start in your own classroom if the school culture is unsympathetic - or to make a start in one school if the system as a whole is unsympathetic - or how to make a start in education if the whole national culture is unsympathetic. All these issues were aired and briefly discussed and in addition the dilemma posed to the liberal reformer wanting to be more democratic when confronted by fundamentalism of various kinds - a real life daily experience for several participants faced with young people who had been brought up to have ears only for the issues of concern to their own religious or 'racial' group.

Conclusion

The workshop concluded with agreement that the task was daunting but that bright sparks of hope existed, often in unlikely places, and that it was important to share information much more systematically. Two final statements emerged:-

• There needs to be much more research into the democratisation of schools on a worldwide basis and that the fruits of that research need to be more effectively disseminated.

• You have to start where you are and not wait for the time or the environment to be 'just right' - it never will be!

References

Atkinson, R. (1994) *Radical Urban Solutions*, London, Cassell.

Caulkin, S. (1993) 'The Boy from Brazil', *Observer*, 17.10.93.

Colbert, V. et al. (1993) 'The New School Program: More and Better Primary Education for Children in Rural Areas in Colombia', in: H.M. Levin and M.E. Lockheed (Eds.) *Effective Schools in Developing Countries*, London, Falmer.

Corbett, A. (1994) 'The Continuing Saga of Lifelong Learning', *Times Education Supplement*, 15.7.94.

Dearing, Sir R. (1994) *The National Curriculum:Final Report*, London, School Curriculum and Assessment Authority.

Department for Education (1993) *Education Act*, London, HMSO.

Eklov, B., and Dneprov, R. (1993) *Democracy in the Russian School*, Oxford, Westview and Boulder Press.

Etzioni. A. (1983) 'It's time to make Responsibility the First R!', *Instructor*, 93, pp. 78-79.

Florida Department of Education (1992) *Blueprint 2000: System of School Improvement and Accountability*, Tallahassee, Florida Dept. of Education.

Fogelman, K. (1991) 'Citizenship in Secondary Schools: The National Picture', in K. Fogelman (Ed) *Citizenship In Schools*, London, Fulton.

Fullan, M. (1982) *The Meaning of Educational Change*, London, Cassell.

Fullan, M. (1991) *The New Meaning of Educational Change*, London, Cassell.

Gilbert, R. (1994) 'Identity, Culture and Environment: Education for Citizenship for the Twenty-First Century', in J. Demaine and H. Entwhistle (Eds) *Citizenship, Politics and Education*, (In preparation).

Gray, P. and Chanoff, D. (1986) 'Democratic Schooling: What Happens to Young People Who Have Charge of their Own Education?', *American Journal of Education*, Feb. 1986, pp. 182-213.

Handy, C. (1984) *Taken for Granted? Looking at Schools as Organisations*, London, Longman.

Hannam, D.H. (1992) *Curriculum Development in the Arts: An Evaluation of the Derbyshire Programme*, M.Phil. dissertation, Exeter University.

Hannam, D.H. (1993) 'Arts and the Adolescent Revisited', in: M. Ross (Ed) *Wasteland Wonderland: The Arts in the National Curriculum*, Exeter, University of Exeter.

Hargreaves, D. and Hopkins, D. (1991) *School Development Planning*, London, Cassell.

Harvey Jones, Sir J. (1994) 'Sir John Seeks Revolution', interviewed in *Times Educational Supplement*, 8.7.94.

Keys, W. and Fernandes, C. (1993) *What Do Students Think About School*, Slough, NFER.

Kohlberg, L. (1985) 'A Just Community Approach to Moral Education' in Theory and Practice, in: M. Berkowitz and F. Oser (Eds) *Moral Education: Theory and Practice*, New Jersey, Lawrence Erlbaum.

Leask, M. (1992) 'A Whole School Approach to Planning', in: G.Wallace (Ed) *Local Management of Schools*, BERA Dialogues No. 6, Clevenon, Multi-Lingual Matters.

Lucas, B. (1994) 'Grounds for Celebration', *Times Educational Supplement*, 26.8.94.

Lynch,J. (1992) *Education for Citizenship in a Multicultural Society*, London, Cassell.

Meighan, R. and Toogood, P. (1992) *Anatomy of Choice in Education*, Ticknall, Education Now Books.

Morgan, R. (1993) *School Life: Pupil's Views on Boarding*, London, HMSO.

Mortimore, P., et al., (1988) *School Matters: The Junior Years*, Somerset, Open Books.

National Association for Pastoral Care in Education (1993) *Whole Curriculum Co-ordination: Time for a New Impetus*, NAPCE response to SCAA National Curriculum Revision Proposals, NAPCE, Education Department, University of Warwick.

O'Connor, M. (1994) *Giving Parents a Voice*, London, The Research and Information on State Education Trust.

Office for Standards in Education (1994) *Handbook for the Inspection of Schools*, London, HMSO.

Oser, F. (1992) 'Three Paths Towards a Just Community: The German Experience', *Moral Education Forum*, Jan 1992, pp. 2-5.

Patemen, C. (1970) *Participation and Democratic Theory*, Cambridge, Cambridge University Press.

Power, C. (1985) 'Democratic Moral Education in the Large High School', in: M. Berkowitz and F. Oser (Eds) *Moral Education: Theory and Practice*, New Jersey, Lawrence Erlbaum.

Power, C. (1988) The Just Community Approach to Moral Education, *Journal of Moral Education*, 17, pp. 195-208.

Rogacheva, A. (1994) 'The Democratisation in the Classroom', paper prepared for the International Conference on Democracy in Schools, Copenhagen, 27-29 October 1994.

Rutter, M., et al. (1979) *Fifteen Thousand Hours: Secondary Schools and their Effects on Children*, London, Open Books.

Semler, R. (1992) *Maverick,* London, Century.

Sizer, T. (1986) 'Rebuilding: First Steps by the Coalition of Essential Schools', *Phi Delta Kappan*, Sept. 1986, pp. 38-42.

Undervisnings Ministeriet (1993) *Education in Denmark:The Folkskole*, Copenhagen, Royal Danish Ministry of Education and Research.

Wilson, B. and Corcoran, T. (1988) *Successful Secondary Schools: Visions of Excellence in American Public Education*, Philadelphia, Falmer Press.

Zalaznick, E. (1980) 'The Just Community School:A Student Perspective', *Moral Education Forum*, 5, pp. 27-35.

Democratising further education

by Frank Reeves

Introduction

The Education Reform Act 1988 and the Further and Higher Education Act 1992 established a new statutory, fiscal, and decision-making framework for further education and fundamentally changed the nature of the relationship of further education colleges to the local communities they served.

The Acts radically altered, in two stages, the formal mechanisms of governance and control of colleges, strengthened the influence of employers at the expense of other interests, and effectively removed the already tenuous grip of locally elected or nominated individuals on further education policy and practice. By 1993, a new market model had been introduced consisting of a major national purchaser of education and training in the form of a Further Education Funding Council (for England) and about 450 further education and sixth-form colleges.

Education Reform Act

The Education Reform Act provided a new statutory definition of further education, introduced schemes for local authority strategic planning and formula-funding of further education, gave colleges greater control over the appointment and dismissal of teaching and non-teaching staff, and changed the composition and role of college governing bodies. While colleges gained a greater degree of freedom from the local authority through the delegation of financial and other responsibilities, the local authority continued as the legal employer of college staff and to exercise control over the college budget.

The local authority was expected to review on an annual basis the contribution that each college should make to the existing pattern of provision in order to ensure it met the local area's changing student and employer needs. The implementation of schemes of delegation tended to become less of an exercise in strategic planning and more one of sharing out a limited, locally-agreed, LEA further-education budget between colleges. A separation of functions had occurred; the local authority was now purchaser and the college was provider.

The Education Reform Act also altered the composition and reduced the size of college governing bodies, action justified on the grounds that such bodies should be independent, be *balanced* in their membership, and play a part in determining the direction of the institution.

Most critically, the Act provided that at least half of college governors should be drawn from business, industry, the professions, and other employment interests (including trade unionists and practitioners in areas relevant to the work of the college). In order to guarantee independence from the Local Education Authority, LEA membership was limited to one fifth of the total number - not more than 4 in a body of 20. In addition to the college principal's place, remaining places might be filled by one student representative, two staff representatives (teaching and non-teaching) and representatives of community bodies, neighbouring educational institutions, or parents. Once the first generation of employment interest governors had been selected for a four-year term by local bodies (approved by the Secretary of State for Education), any subsequent vacancies were to be filled by further nominations of these bodies.

The effect was threefold: a cut in the overall size of the governing body, an increase in the employment interest set up as a self-perpetuating oligarchy, and a reduction in the influence of the LEA. This last was the government's specifically stated intention.

Further and Higher Education Act

The Further and Higher Education Act of 1992 resulted in the removal of approximately 450 further education, tertiary, sixth-form, agricultural, and art and design colleges from local authority control and the setting up of funding councils, one for England and one for Wales, to create a nationally funded system of further education.

The Further Education Funding Council for England - a non-departmental public body (NDPB), more frequently referred to as a quasi-autonomous non-governmental agency (or QUANGO), has fourteen members (not less than 12 not more than 15) appointed by the Secretary of State for Education who also appoints its chair. The council's main responsibilities are to allocate government resources to colleges and to secure adequate further education provision. The government has set the council the task of improving efficiency, encouraging colleges to seek funding from private sources, providing incentives for expansion in student numbers, supporting provision for students with learning difficulties, stabilising funding, and making funding allocations conditional on the delivery of a specified level of service.

One of the government's main aims for the council has been to support the drive to improve the level of education and training of the work force by providing opportunities to gain qualifications within the new national vocational qualification framework (NVQs). In terms of public accountability, the council places great store on systems of financial control, auditing, obtaining value for money, and safeguarding the public purse.

Targets for further education and training are now decided at national level with the council funding mechanism acting as the incentive for individual colleges to achieve those targets.   Only students following courses with recognised qualification aims - vocational or academic - qualify for funding.

Purchasing

The council claims that it has three kinds of relationship with colleges: advisory, developmental, and prescriptive.   In practice, it has achieved a virtually unchallenged control over the sector and its direction of development by requiring all colleges to comply with the conditions it attaches to the funding it dispenses - which constitutes by far the largest part of most colleges' budgets (although there are other minor purchasers as mentioned below).   The Further Education Funding Council is effectively a sole buyer - in a position to dictate the price of what it purchases, rather like the diamond-buying arm of De Beers.

There are other possible purchasers of college services, for example, employers, Training and Enterprise Councils, individual private users, and local authorities (the last may support non-vocational leisure, or non-schedule 2 courses, not funded by the FEFC).   Frank Coffield (1990), however, has observed that "training is perceived by many employers as a disposable overhead dropped at the first sign of lowering profit margins", and the proportion of full-cost education and training in colleges paid for by employers is small.

Training and Enterprise Councils (which can buy training from colleges but are not, in general, major college customers) are companies limited by guarantee, run by boards of directors, two thirds of whom are senior managers from the private sector and the other third drawn from local authorities, trade unions, the voluntary sector, and other bodies.

Apart from local authority councillors, none of the members of the formal decision-making bodies of the main corporate purchasers of further education is directly elected or publicly accountable to local populations. The application of the purchaser/provider market model transfers responsibility for further education, conceptually and practically, from the political sphere to the economic sphere, in the context of a liberal democratic state in which direct political intervention in the working of private enterprise ·and the market is regarded as unacceptable.

Colleges as providers

Once the parameters for funding have been set by the major purchaser, colleges are permitted some scope in how they are to achieve the numerical targets (now measured in funding units) on which their budget depends.

Under the Further and Higher Education Act 1992, colleges became corporations. The corporation must have no less than 10, but not more than 20 members. At least half should be business members (that is engaged or employed in business, industry, professions, or field of employment relevant to the activities of the institution). Significantly, all former local authority nominations and appointments were excluded from membership.

The corporation is intended to be smaller in size than a governing body and to be composed, not of representatives or delegates, but of independent individuals acting in their own right and being forbidden to speak or vote on mandates from outside bodies. The reformed college is not accountable, nor intended to be, to any local community. Rather, it is expected to respond to the quasi-market forces exercised by the Further Education Funding Council in pursuit of the government's national education and training priority expressed, for example, by the government-established National Training Task Force and its National Targets for Education and Training (DFE, 1992).

Powers of college corporations

The corporation takes on many of the tasks previously performed by the local education authority and is responsible for determining the educational character and mission of the college, overseeing college activities, the effective and efficient use of college resources, the college's solvency, the safeguarding of its assets, approval of annual estimates of income and expenditure, the remuneration and hiring and firing of senior post-holders, and setting the framework for staff pay and conditions of service.

The chief executive, on the other hand, has responsibility for making proposals about the institution's educational character and mission, for its organisation, direction and management, for the appointment and dismissal of all (apart from senior) staff, determining academic activities, preparing annual estimates of income and expenditure (for corporation approval), managing the budget, and maintaining student discipline including student expulsion. The new emphasis is on financial control, and also the power of the chief executive to manage staff.

The academic board remains as a distinctive feature of further education colleges, but its role is limited to advising the chief executive on the college's academic work. Further education colleges are no longer conceived, albeit idealistically, as communities of independent scholars, exercising democratic autonomy over academic matters. College staff are employers, forming part of a system of educational productivity measured in terms of input and throughput of students and output of qualifications.

Each college is an independent, non-departmental public body providing a further education and training service with an organisational form deliberately modelled on a private sector commercial company. Local council committee meetings were public - college corporations have usually chosen to hold their proceedings in private, in the manner of a company board meeting.

Employee relations

The immediate governance of the further education college is only part of the total picture of the move towards oligarchic control in further education. When colleges were part of the local authority the conditions of service of college staff were negotiated collectively at national and local level between local authorities and recognised trade unions. The consensual practices which allowed the main further education teachers' union, NATFHE, some say in college decisions over pay, conditions and other general matters, have been replaced by a management drive to impose, unilaterally if necessary, new and more stringent contracts of employment with the predictable collapse of earlier collaboration and partnership between college senior staff and lecturers.

The move has been fortified by the recently formed Colleges' Employers' Forum, government public sector pay policy supported by a claw-back mechanism, and the Funding Council's remorseless drive to standardise and reduce unit costs through the exercise of the funding mechanism.   Colleges have become more like business organisations not only in formal structure, but in the more authoritarian nature of the relations between managers and employees.

Role of students

Students, the majority group in colleges, have also been affected by college incorporation.   While still recognised in the formal governance of most institutions, students have suffered from the government's separate attempt to restrict the scope of student union activities and the general authoritarian and anti-union climate of the times.

Despite the charter movement (DFE, 1993), such is the political climate that the users of further education are more likely to be seen not as the students, but as the government, funding council, training and enterprise board, or local industry, which pay directly or indirectly for the college output of skilled labour.   The students' status is determined by their value in the labour market which, in an era of high unemployment, particularly for unqualified young adults, is small.

The curriculum

Higher education institutions have control over the curriculum and accreditation, providing them with some measure of local autonomy.   The curriculum and accreditation in further education is determined in large part by external examination boards (such as the GCE boards, BTEC and C&G) and the National Council for Vocational Qualifications with its national qualification framework and vocational qualifications (NVQs).   Lead bodies, responsible for particular vocational areas, are again dominated by employers.

Conclusion

This completes the picture of a further education transformed in less than five years from a local service run for a range of interests as a tripartite partnership between the local authority, business and college staff, student, and community representatives, to one run locally by a majority business interest as part of a national scheme to improve business productivity and occupational skills. The former elected stakeholders to governing bodies in the form of the local authority have been removed altogether, while the number and power of the staff, student, and community stakeholders have been reduced in favour of the majority business interest, which may replace itself without democratic accountability.

As the main purchaser of college provision, the national Funding Council has a membership appointed by the Secretary of State for Education and in theory is answerable through her/him to parliament. The challenge to policy makers and further education is to devise ways of democratising the sector in the new and developing context: reversion to the old structure is neither feasible, nor likely to advance the cause of democracy.

References

Association of Colleges for Further and Higher Education (ACFHE) (1992), *Further education after the general election, the policies of six political parties*, Swindon, ACFHE and Staff College.

Bash, L. and Coulby, D. (1989), *The Education Reform Act, Competition and Control*, London, Cassell.

Coffield, F. (1990) "From the decade of the enterprise culture to the decade of the TECs" in *British Journal of Education and Work* 4(i), pp. 59-78.

Department for Education (1993), *Further choice and quality, the Charter for Further Education*, London, DFE., and,
(1992), *National Education and Training Targets*, London, DFE.

Department of Education and Science (1988), *Education Reform Act 1988, Government of Maintained Further and Higher Education Colleges*, Circular /88), London, DES., and,
1988), *Education Reform Act 1988: local management of further and higher education colleges: planning and delegation schemes and articles of government*, (Circular 9/88), London, DES., and,
(1987), *Maintained Further Education: financing, governance and law*, London, DES.

Department of Education and Science and Welsh Office (1987), *Managing Colleges Efficiently. Report of a Study of Efficiency in Non-advanced Further Education,* for the Government and the Local Authority Associations, London, HMSO.

Department of Education and Science, Department of Employment, and Welsh Office (1991), *Education and Training for the Twenty-first Century,* Vols 1 and 2 (Comnd 1536, May 1991), London, HMSO.

Further Education Campaign Group (1993), *A New Manifesto for a New Era,* Solihull, FECG.

Further Education Funding Council (1992), *Funding Learning,* Coventry, FEFC., and
(1994), *Guide for College Governors,* Coventry, FEFC.

Further Education Unit (1993), *Challenges for Colleges: Developing a corporate approach to curriculum and strategic planning,* London, FEU.

HMSO (1994), *Competitiveness: Helping Business to Win* and
(1992), *Further and Higher Education Act 1992,* Ch. 13. and
(1988), *Education Reform Act 1988,* Ch. 40. London, HMSO.

Industry Matters (1988), *New Governors for Further Education, Information for industry and commerce,* London, Industry Matters.

National Council for Vocational Qualifications (1988), NCVQ *Information Leaflets,* London, NCVQ.

Smithers, A. and Robinson, P. (1993), *Changing Colleges, Further Education in the Market Place,* London, Council for Industry and Higher Education.

Taylor-Gooby, P. and Lawson, R. (eds) (1993), *Markets and Managers, New Issues in the Delivery of Welfare.* Buckingham, Open University.

Wymer, K. (1992), *Further Education Colleges, the New Context,* occasional paper, Wolverhampton, Bilston Community College.

The Preparation of Prospective Teachers
and the Strange Case of Democracy in Action

by Roland Meighan and Janet Meighan

Introduction

> *"The schools of education throughout the country where young people receive their pre-service and in-service training are, by and large, in a sorry state. They tend to be rigid bastions of conventional thinking and practice and highly resistant to change."* *(Rogers, 1983, p. 163)*

In making this observation, the educational psychologist Carl Rogers was writing about the situation in the USA. He went on to say that students in his country had, for the most part, come to regard the courses as a boring waste of time. These comments echo similar things often said about the situation in the UK.

This situation is not divorced from the experience of the USA education system as a whole or the UK system in general, which another USA writer, E.T. Hall, suggests has:

> *"... transformed learning from one of the most rewarding of all human activities into a painful, boring, dull, fragmenting, mind-shrinking, soul-shrivelling experience."* *(Hall, 1977, p. 102)*

Carl Rogers is able to report that he did encounter exceptions where:

> *"... a human climate for learning is created, where prospective teachers experience the excitement of discovery - both in regard to themselves and the subject matter they will teach. They find it rewarding to be part of a dual process - the process of becoming more of themselves, and the process of promoting and facilitating learning in their students."* *(Rogers, 1983, p. 163)*

(In the UK the kind of exceptions Rogers described used to be found in courses for the preparation of Primary school teachers and in particular in some Early

Childhood courses. Tutors of such courses now struggle against an onslaught of regressive legislation.)

It is perhaps hard to explain the feeling of relief these comments from the USA can bring after many years of trying to cope with similar conclusions about teacher education in UK and trying to provide something more effective for prospective teachers.

The other source of relief has been the positive reaction of the students, (see Harber and Meighan, 1989) who after experiencing a democratically-run course themselves, can write comments in their course evaluations to the effect that:

> "There was intellectual enjoyment.   Intellectual exploration became an exciting and satisfying end in its own right, rather than as a means to a boring and worthless end, e.g. exams, assessment, the teacher's aims, etc."

> "The co-operative spent many hours in discussion and formulated opinions and views (often varying) in relation to our timetable of work. All the group members felt without any reservation whatsoever that the co-op was a new working experience which was stimulating, enjoyable and very worth while."

The students making these observations had chosen a non-authoritarian mode for their initial teacher education course - a democratic learning co-operative.

A vision and a decision

So, what happens in a democratic approach to a teacher education course?   A similar pattern emerged in the various courses for which the authors were responsible. After a short settling-in period, when the students had introduced each other to the group, the news was broken that although the tutor had a planned course ready in the familiar authoritarian expert style, there were other options open to the group.   They could consider operating as a democratic learning co-operative that devised and planned its own programme of studies using the tutors as resources if and when deemed appropriate.   A specimen contract (see appendix) was available for discussion purposes if this option required any elaboration.   (In one institution they could also opt for an individualised course based on an individual tutorial system as used at Oxford and Cambridge.   This is the solo learner-managed possibility.)   But the decision was to be made by them, because replacing a compulsory authoritarian course with a compulsory democratic one, was not the idea.

The course thus began as a consultation about the approach to be adopted for the course itself.   There was, in fact, another option made available to the group and that was of a mixture of approaches, e.g. adopting one approach for one term and another for another term, or some members choosing an individualised course if the majority want either a lecturer-taught course or a learning co-operative.

Students had an initial experience working in schools and further teaching practices during their course. These provided a wealth of ideas, insights and questions from which they could construct a course and review the initial plans in the light of further experience.

There is a need to clarify what 'a course' actually meant. In one case it referred to the 'methods of teaching' module of their Post Graduate Certificate of Education year, taking up about one third of their total time, and these particular students had social studies (economics, politics and sociology) and humanities as their subject goal. The number in the groups varied from year to year, from twelve to twenty. In another case it referred to the curriculum module which was part of the preparation of teachers of young children. (Elsewhere, courses preparing teachers for Business Studies have been involved - see Harber and Meighan 1989, Section two, Chapter 7).

Seventeen years of experience

Courses covered a period of seventeen years in two different institutions. In two cases the lecturer taught course was selected for one part of the course and a democratic learning co-operative for another part. One course elected to begin with a taught course for a week or two as a period of familiarisation and then to change to a co-operative approach. The other courses have adopted the learning co-operative option from the outset. The learning co-operative experience has been externally monitored, once by an independent university evaluator and twice during visitations by a team of Her Majesty's Inspectors. It has also been regularly monitored by the annual visits of external examiners.

The tutors had to adjust to a different theory of teaching and so did most of the students. Tutors and most of the students had been educated in one or other of the authoritarian styles where the majority of the decisions had been made for them rather than by them. They were used to being either the anvil or the hammer.

The tutors had to learn :

- to listen much more than they had been used to, and learn to resist their previous habits of dominating the decision-making,

- to cope with the anxiety aroused when their expertise was sometimes seen to be less significant than they had previously supposed,

- to trust the learners to apply their intelligence in planning and executing a course. This was against all the previous training of both students and tutors and in opposition to the strongly held beliefs of most colleagues that the intelligence of students could not be relied on,

- to cope with the anxiety of sharing power,
  (There was considerable irony in feeling anxious at having helped students to manage competently on their own when this exactly what they would need to do for the duration of their careers. Were we really earning our money by facilitation rather than instruction ?)

- to cope with the tasks of facilitation which proved to be demanding in identifying sources, making contacts, and solving operational problems on the spot or at short notice: this helped satisfy our Protestant Work Ethic habituation. The easier authoritarian option of preparing handouts and resources well in advance suddenly seemed very comfortable, safe and strangely appealing.

The students had to learn:

- to cope with being active rather than passive: to accept the idea that since teaching was primarily a decision-making activity, the way to learn might be to simulate the process using themselves as guinea pigs by selecting the aims, content, methods, and evaluations for their own learning. Previous experience had an influence here :

"We all felt that the work that we had been engaged upon for our first degree courses had been too competitive and too isolated. Therefore we all agreed that something else had to be attempted for our year within the faculty."

- to take responsibility for their own and others learning. This was seen as improving standards in contrast to the predictions of colleagues that students would not devise the 'best' course :

"With all students choosing the range of subjects, the content, inevitably (in my mind), was of a greater range and of more relevance than if the 'teacher' had done all the choosing. A group of students, especially from different specialist backgrounds, was able to provide more resources that one teacher could."

- to acquire both techniques for teaching in schools as they were, alongside a vision of future possibilities:

"The course, in practice, seemed to me to cope nicely with the idealism of educational change and the practicalities and constraints involved in operationalising such changes.   In this way the course provided a realistic 'vision' for changed procedures in teaching whilst not ignoring the problems of practice, or survival, which face all teachers."

- to cope with the realisation that they were able to motivate themselves after all:

"I felt great responsibility for the course and this involvement meant always taking a mentally active part.   I felt no resentment against somebody trying to impose work or a situation on me. Thus motivation was high."

Solo and collective learner-managed learning in partnership

The stress in this account has all been on the collective aspect of the learning. In reality, the courses required the development of both the solo type of learner-managed and the collective form, in interaction with each other.   The groups used the device of allocating tasks to individuals, and sometimes pairs and trios, which required them to go off and research and prepare material, activities and sessions. The results of their solo activities would then be fed back into the group programme.

The tutors were part of the group and their experience was available to the group at any time. Groups frequently requested tutors to lead particular sessions as part of the programme. Tutors could also voice an opinion or contribute ideas but needed to learn to do this sparingly. They could afford to be patient and reserve many contributions they might make because the process of collective planning, doing and reviewing had strong self-correcting tendencies.

Better or worse teachers?

There was initially apprehension about how students involved in a democratic learning co-operative would fare on teaching practice, with job applications and with interviews. Such apprehension is now a thing of the past. Students used to making decisions about what to learn, assembling appropriate materials and using them with a selected method and then evaluating the outcome, tend to transfer these behaviours to the school situation with some confidence. And being used to working co-operatively, they fitted into a team situations with relative ease. They had also experienced a range of teaching styles within their learning co-operative and had learned to value different approaches.

The feedback from applications for posts and interviews has also denied early apprehension. The approach of the students seem to appeal to many interviewers. Head teachers have been known to phone the tutors with comments like:

> " this is a whole new generation of prospective teachers, articulate, enthusiastic, industrious, and challenging. "

These young teachers were also aware of and experiencing all the three forms of discipline. People sometimes think that discipline is the simple problem of adults making children behave to instructions. This is only one kind of discipline - the authoritarian. Three kinds can be identified. They are:

1. **Authoritarian** - where order is based on rules imposed by adults. Power resides in an individual or group of leaders.
2. **Autonomous** - where order is based on self-discipline and self-imposed rational rules. Power resides with the individual.

3. **Democratic** - where order is based on rules agreed after rational discussion: i.e. based on evidence, human rights values and the logic of consequences. Power is shared amongst the people in the situation.

There has been a centuries-old debate about which of these three is the best system of discipline. It is now a sterile debate. The complexities of modern life are such that all three types of discipline have a place to play in the scheme of things. Sometimes we need to follow instructions or take on leadership roles thus following the authoritarian approach. In an aeroplane, debating who should fly the aircraft and the rules of flying is not the appropriate form of discipline that matches the situation. In a car, the driver needs autonomous discipline and to make the decisions about driving the car without the confusions of being over-ruled by an authoritarian, or advised by a committee of back-seat drivers.

In many other situations, 'several heads are likely to be better than one' in deciding the rules to be adopted, based on the evidence and the rights of all involved. Power-sharing, although time-consuming, is then likely to lead to better, fairer, and agreed decisions with co-operative system of order.

It follows that there are three types of error as regards discipline. One, the current error of most UK schooling, is to select the authoritarian as the predominant approach. The second, the error of some radical thinkers, is to make the autonomous the One Right Way. The third error from another radical tradition, is to make the democratic the exclusive approach. All these One Right Way approaches fail to match the need for young people to learn what most of their elders have clearly failed to learn, that is, how to be competent in the logistics and practice of all three types of discipline, and to select them appropriately.

The young teachers learning by means of the democratic approach developed the flexibility to use each form of discipline as appropriate within their course, and later, within their own practise as teachers.

Towards giving prospective teachers curiosity, courage, confidence and criticism.

In contrast to the remarks of Hall quoted earlier about learning being turned into a mind shrinking and soul shrivelling experience, James Hemming (1984), an independent and eminent educational psychologist, has argued that some of the key characteristics of successful education are the three Cs of curiosity, courage and confidence to which he adds a fourth, that of criticism in the sense of self-evaluation. The approach through offering the experience of learning co-operatives to prospective teachers has encouraged us to see this as a step in the direction of such achievements. It would be foolish, however, to overstate the claims. The writers are all too aware of the observations about the limitations of democratic approaches:

"So, two cheers for democracy: one because it admits variety and two because it permits criticism. Two cheers are quite enough: there is no occasion to give three." E.M. Forster

"Democracy is the worst system of organisation - except for all the others." Winston Churchill

The implication of Churchill's observation is, however, that if you do not have a democratic approach **you are bound to have something worse!**

Appendix: A Group Learning Contract

We agree to accept responsibility for our course as a group.

We agree to take an active part in the learning of the group.

We agree to be constructively critical of our own and other people's ideas.

We agree to plan our own programme of studies, implement it using the group members and appointed teachers as resources, and review the outcomes in order that we may learn from any limitations we identify.

We agree to the keeping of a group log-book of work completed, planning decisions, session papers and any other appropriate documents.

We agree to share the duties of being in the chair, the task of being meeting secretary and the roles of session organisers and contributors.

We agree to review this contract from time to time.

References

Chamberlin, R. (1989) *Free Children and Democratic Schools* London: Falmer

Davies, L. (1994) *Beyond Authoritarian School Management* Ticknall: Education Now Books.

Engle, S. and Ochoa, A. (1989) *Education for Democratic Citizenship* Columbia: Teachers College Press.

Gordon, T. (1986) *Democracy in one School?* London: Falmer.

Hall, E. T. (1977) *Beyond Culture* New York: Doubleday.

Harber, C., and Meighan, R., (1989) *The Democratic School: Educational Management and the Practice of Democracy* Ticknall: Education Now Books.

Harber, C. (1992) *Democratic Learning and Learning Democracy* Ticknall: Education Now Books.

Hemming, J. (1984) "The Confidence-building Curriculum" in Harber C.et.al. (1984) *Alternative Educational Futures* London: Holt Rhinehart and Winston.

Meighan, R. (1986) *A Sociology of Educating* (second edition) London: Cassell.

Meighan, R. (1988) *Flexischooling* Ticknall: Education Now Books.

Meighan, R. (1994) *The Freethinkers' Guide to the Educational Universe* Nottingham: Educational Heretics Press.

Rogers, C. (1983) *Freedom to Learn for the Eighties* Colombus, Ohio: Merrill.

Nicholls, J. G. (1989) *The Competitive Ethos and Democratic Education* Cambridge Massachusetts: Harvard University Press.

White, P. (1983) *Beyond Domination* London: Routledge and Kegan Paul.

Democratising Higher Education

by Patrick Ainley

Introduction

There are two interconnected problems facing the democratisation of higher education. One is the general one that faces us all at any level of education, or indeed in any of the public services today. That is how to prevent the privatisation and dismantling of the welfare state and bring public services back under public control. This will require a resolutely decentralised reform in terms of the management and local control of the welfare state - even though its financing will still involve national redistribution according to priority of need.

Like other public institutions, democratic control of universities, colleges and schools by their staffs and students must be reasserted, together with their responsibility to local (city-wide or regional) democratic structures. Vocational education must also be rescued from the market place - abolishing Training and Enterprise Councils and making all public expenditure on education and training publicly accountable to democratically elected bodies.

Having sorted all that out (!), the second and particular problem of higher education has to be confronted. This is the part that higher education plays in legitimating what has been called the 'official knowledge' of society. Not only what is accepted as scientifically valid and historically established scholarship but, more importantly, the part that higher education - particularly Oxbridge - plays in endorsing the rule of unaccountable elites.

From elite to mass higher eduation

For elite higher education represents not only the social ideal of the ruling class, for whom private schools lead effortlessly via Oxbridge to positions of influence and power, it also validates the antidemocratic practices of elite professionalism. For throughout the century with the growth of higher education, degrees have become necessary for entry to a range of occupations which have closed themselves off from non-graduate applicants. Thus, alongside 'the working class', a whole 'thinking class' has grown up, dealing in more or less abstract knowledge, especially in the media and advertising but also in teaching and research. The training for employment of this 'thinking class' includes the higher education that develops high levels of literacy together with general reasoning abilities.

This division between those who decide and those who do, between professionals and their clients, as well as between those who know (or think they know) and those who do not (or who think they do not) is now breaking down, along with the arbitrary divisions of academic specialisms. Partly this is happening under the impact of new technology that potentially makes information available to all. It is also occurring due to the reformation of social classes and the restructuring of work organisations and the state faced with accelerating economic decline and the loss of heavy industry.

The same social forces have now brought the majority of school leavers, as well as many adults, into some sort of Further and Higher Education. The latest expansion of F and HE along the American model may present itself as a professionalisation of the proletariat but in the reality of education without jobs and hyper-inflation of qualifications it is really a proletarianisation of the professions. Expansion is however unstoppable, even if only hesitantly and half-heartedly pursued by a government who do not fund it adequately and by the majority of academics who oppose what they regard as the contradiction of 'mass higher education'.

Moreover, the expansion of F/HE affords great opportunities for democracy in education. For the fundamental cultural activity, if society is to be reconstructed from the bottom up, is democratic debate and decision making. Thus we cannot return to the professional paradigm of the welfare state in which educated professionals acted on behalf of ignorant clients. Instead, we have to move forward to a democratic alternative to the market in which knowledge and power are shared in a new division of labour mixing manual and mental work with the new technology that makes this possible.

For education, science and the arts therefore, the first priority is to re-establish their central purpose: to stimulate thought and develop new knowledge and skills to deal with a rapidly changing reality.

Polyconceptualists not monotechnicians

This requires a new curriculum at all levels of education; one that will be democratically decided upon by those involved in learning. The hold of academic elitism over the entire system can be broken practically only by, as Eric Robinson wrote in 1968 in his book on 'The New Polytechnics', `breaking the domination of the whole educational system by universities which are devoted to the academic ideal.' Turning Oxbridge into residential adult colleges would be widely supported by the many people who would then be given a chance to attend such colleges. It would also nip in the bud the present moves towards setting up a super-league of semi-private elite institutions preserving their privileged position through marketing archaic and elite courses to those able to pay for them.

The ending of the binary divide between universities and polytechnics plus colleges would not then result in widening the social divisions within higher education and creating new academic divisions. Instead of the polytechnics aping the universities as they are now attempting to do, the original polytechnic vision of popular universities ought to be spread throughout the new unified higher education sector. It is less polytechnicians, however, who are required nowadays, than polyconceptualists.

Polyconceptualism requires a pedagogical approach that begins by examining the situation of students and staff in education and in society, building up from the particular to the general and facilitating transfer between them via independent study. Students could then be afforded opportunities to think by not only sorting information into established categories but questioning those categories to establish their own classifications and orderings of knowledge.

This would lead to a real empowerment of learners and teachers, rather than the rhetoric of empowerment through consumer choice of modules in the market place. The limits of such 'student empowerment' was shown by the simultaneous attempts by government to abolish the only democratic representation that students enjoy through the National Union of Students.

To introduce elements of democratic debate and determination to all courses is easier said than done. It is, however, a goal which should inform all relations between teachers and taught and the active, independent and collaborative methods of learning and assessment that are adopted.

Individual students can then not only subject their own hypotheses, ideas and claims to truth generally to the relevant criteria, whether of scientific experiment, logical proof, social research or technical practice. They can also defend the conclusions they arrived at in argument with fellow students, teachers and others. They can therefore acknowledge the point at which their truth claims no longer depend upon proof but are a statement of faith or an admission of prejudice. Nor can they deny that their thought is in some sense ideological, that it is - as well as a more of less adequate conception of the reality with which they are dealing - expressive of an interest in or perspective upon that reality which it represents.

Moreover, that which position they choose to take is, as well as an aesthetic, logical or practical choice, also a moral or political decision that may require democratic endorsement as well as rational agreement to find a wider acceptance. Such discussion can be encouraged by teachers in collaborative learning with students. It can be institutionalised through learning contracts between the students and staff of institutions in which mutually negotiated courses of study will include elements of independent study developed by individual and group learning on socially useful projects. The nature and range of this learning will be limited only by the needs and imaginations of the participants and costs will be lessened by the social usefulness of this practical knowledge.

The new further and higher continuing education

The new higher education curriculum should therefore include as large an element as possible of independent study in the degree programmes of all students. Instead of 'cramming' for tests that select a minority for entry to the next stage, the methods of learning and assessment associated with primary project work and GCSE course work before it was restricted by government should be raised and made continuous from the schools through to further and higher education. In a complementary motion, the independent scholarship, research and creation of post-graduate learning should be brought down and integrated into all pre-graduate courses.

At present only art students are assessed exclusively or mainly on their creative efforts. Yet creation, investigation, experiment and debate by all students and as many other people as possible is vital today when so many received ideas in the social and natural sciences are open to question.

In addition, new technology can be applied at every level of learning to facilitate routine memorisation and allow imagination free reign beyond the immediate necessity to earn a wage and the constraints of production for profit. This space within education for seeding new ideas must be preserved and extended by making research and creation an integral part of the independent study of all students, rather than separating teaching from research as the government now proposes.

Independent and individual study across traditional subject boundaries can be facilitated by the widely proposed and implemented modular systems of certification. These facilitate access through various modes of part-time and distance learning at home and at work. They also enable credit accumulation and transfer and the recognition of prior experience. They permit entry and exit points from diploma level on through certificate to degree and masters level that can ease the present long, full-time slog to qualification.

In a modular system, however, it is essential not to lose sight of the divisions between disciplines as well as the inter-relations between them. It is therefore important to distinguish between 'genuine' fields of study and practice corresponding to defined areas of reality on the one hand, and on the other, outdated and arbitrary academic subject divisions, which only hinder thought and dampen discovery.

Whilst advances in knowledge often come from the imaginative projection from one frame of reference to another, this is not the same as a 'pick-n-mix' of modules from different areas of study. Guided only by vocational (ie. labour market) choice, there is a loss of theoretical generalised knowledge and skill in favour of specialised information and competence applicable only to occupational tasks not conceptually related to one another. Philosophical discussion, counselling and support is therefore required if the modular method is not to degenerate into irrelevant educational consumerism in traditional elite higher education institutions at one end of the hierarchy, combined with the myopic relevance of narrow vocational goals in mass institutions at the other.

Nor should modularisation become a way of just processing more students, as it already has in some former-polytechnics and in many of the longer established universities that have become like them.

The first step to generalise the knowledge to inform democratic modernisation is to establish for as many people as possible the normality and desirability of full-time education to 18 and recurring returns to learning full- and part-time thereafter. This entitlement should also be used to emphasise the assumption of full citizenship rights and responsibilities for all from the age of 18, instead of relegating a section of youth to a secondary labour market.

For those alienated by their previous schooling, a further two years in sixth form or college may have little resemblance to their previous schooling - which in any case will have to change, doing away with the outdated and academic 'National' Curriculum and its associated tests and league tables. Like education at all levels, learning experiences must be personally meaningful and life-enhancing, developed in relation to the cultures of the local population and linking knowledge and skills to what people already know and can do.

Adequate financial support should also be available to students from 16 onwards to raise participation rates and return post-18. Student loans must be abolished as this only deters people unwilling to become indebted from continuing education. With a progressive tax system, graduate taxes are also unnecessary. The Robbins principle should be revived to give right of entry to local college full or part-time, in or out of employment. This should not depend upon an academic judgement of whether the student has the 'ability to benefit' from higher education as judged by their previous academic qualifications. Nor are vouchers necessary to enforce this entitlement, which should be constitutionally and legally enforceable.

If the right of all school leavers to enter their local college is guaranteed, progression from schools and adult education will facilitate access to higher education. For those in and out of employment, further education colleges are well placed to become the linch-pin of the new system. Rather than shorten degree courses, the two years which many students already spend in FE or sixth form before moving on to higher education can become the basis for a new two-plus-two-plus-two year degree structure, the first two years to 18 for standard age entrants leading to a broad-based diploma combining the academic and the vocational. Many diplomates would move on, then or later, to take their study up to degree level with two further years full-time at higher education college, followed by two years post-graduate study to Masters level.

Conclusion

Simply, education at all levels can no longer be about selection for the employment hierarchy. The 'needs' of industry have to be set in a wider framework of human cultural and environmental need. New technology provides the potential to enable all working people to become multiskilled and flexible in a true sense, able to undertake a wide range of specific and general tasks, including self-management of their cooperative enterprises and democratic government of their society.

Only information combined with democracy can provide the knowledge/skills necessary for survival.

The argument of this chapter is exerpted from the author's latest book. (see Ainley, P. below):

References

Ainley, P. (1994) *Degrees of Difference, Higher Education in the 1990s,* London, Lawrence and Wishart.

Barnett, R. (1994) *The Limits of Competence*, Milton Keynes, Open University Press.

Bordieu, P. and Passeron, J. (1979) *The Inheritors, French Students and their Relation to Culture,* Trans R. Nice Chicago, University of Chicago Press.

Evans, C. (1993) *English People, the Experience of Teaching and Learning English in British Universities*, Milton Keynes, Open University Press.

Halsey, A. (1992) *Decline of Donnish Domination, The British Academic Professions in the Twentieth Century*, Oxford, Clarendon Press.

Institute for Public Policy Research (1992) *Higher Education, Expansion and Reform*, London IPPR.

Robbins, D. (1988) *The Rise of Independent Study, the Politics and Philosophy of an Educational Innovation, 1970-87*, Milton Keynes, Open University Press.

Robinson, E. (1968) *The New Polytechnics, the People's Universities*, Harmondsworth, Penguin.

Slater, B. and Tapper, T. (1994) *The State and Higher Education*, London, Woburn Press.

Silver, H. and Brennan, J. (1998) *A Liberal Vocationalism*, London, Methuen.

Thomas, K. (1990) *Gender and Subject in Higher Education*, Milton Keynes, Open University Press.

Setting-up a Democratic Classroom

by Lesley Browne

Introduction

Democratic approaches to learning are a rarity in the British education system. For the last five years, however, Advanced Level Sociology and Politics students at the school where I teach have been given the opportunity to choose how they learn.

After initial discussion about the type of course the students wished to study, they were given a presentation which looked at different methods of learning. The choices included the conventional teacher directed course, a teacher based consultative model, a democratic learning co-operative and an Open University type of course. It was also suggested that a mixture of these options was possible, and that the final alternative might be considered if an individual did not accept the majority view.

These methods of learning have gained support from a HMI Report on the school where I work. The Social Science Department was singled out for particular praise when the HMI (1989) commented that:

> "The lessons observed in the Social and Political studies department were excellent examples of particularly good practice".

The 1989/91 Advanced Level British Government and Politics group illustrates how we introduced the first democratic classroom into a large comprehensive school.

A case study

The aim of setting up a democratic learning environment was to enable young people to take responsibility for their own learning. To enable them to decide their own agenda, then to work individually or in small groups, to prepare lessons, visits, presentations and to organise visiting speakers, etc. Other aims were to increase the students self reliance, to increase confidence, to develop skills of articulation and investigation, and to remove the myth that the teacher is the expert in all things, when there is much that a teacher cannot know and where students have valid experiences and opinions of their own.

However, like Harber and Meighan (1986), I faced an ideological dilemma, because even though one of the aims:

> "*of political education is to encourage a more democratic classroom environment ... is it not undemocratic to force a particular method on students, albeit a democratic one?* ".

Because democracy implies choice, I would argue that wherever possible students should be given the choice of teaching methods, course content and assessment methods. Only when such choices have been given can we claim to have a mandate about how to proceed. As Meighan (1992) points out this is known as the:

> "*pre-democratic, or bridging or authoritarian-consultative regime that represents an attempt to move from an existing authoritarian situation into a democratic without actually sharing much power at that stage.*"

It was decided that for each Advanced Level group in the department the course would be based on choice. At the beginning of the 1989/91 Advanced level Politics course, students were presented with a number of Advanced level Government and Politics syllabuses. These syllabuses ranged from a choice of 100% exam or a mixture of exams and coursework. Students were also given the choice of how to organise their course, as mentioned above.

The initial discussion was an exercise in the important skill of group decision-making. After much debate the 89/91 group - and more recently the 1992/4 group - decided on the democratic model of learning, where the emphasis of the course was to be more collective. I hoped we would be able to create a classroom atmosphere that would promote the procedural values of tolerance, fairness, and openness to change that would encourage student contributions and participation.

The group voiced a general dissatisfaction with the teaching methods they had previously encountered and questioned just how much they had learned in a tutor-led course. The majority felt that this would provide a chance for them to contribute to their own learning experiences. They would develop a sense of responsibility for their own learning and more importantly they would be responsible for each other's learning.

As one of the students commented:

"When we first started the course it came as a bit of a shock. Yeah, it wasn't one of those lessons where you stand at the front and talk for an hour and ten minutes. Its much better than a normal like, er, standard course. It makes you think more, doesn't it, it makes you feel a bit more responsible. If you choose something yourself the emphasis is on you to do well."

Tina said:

"I think its really good. But I think more classes need to be like this. Its more our course. We are teaching each other. You've gotta do it, not the teacher. I'm quite proud of myself like, and its given me more confidence. You don't feel at the bottom, with the teacher at the top. You feel more important when you are asked to choose things like the syllabus. You feel valued and important as a person."

Interestingly, Tina was unconsciously referring to the hidden curriculum here. She highlighted the fact that the social organisation of the school is usually authoritarian and hierarchical and that in fact co-operation and mutual support are disregarded on most courses. She seems to imply that schools could and should do much to alter this situation by encouraging more student participation in the school and community. Education would then have real meaning and impact as the students' activities would be political as well as intellectual. She seems to feel that this has been enhanced for our group, by the development of an open, democratic classroom where they, the students, have power over their own education and the opportunity to develop positive political skills and attitudes.

There was a strong degree of commitment to the course, with most youngsters stating that it has been extremely beneficial both from an academic point of view and a practical point of view. They feel that they have learned a lot and experienced much. As Jamie commented:

"I feel motivated to work and get involved because I feel it is our course".

I would like to use the example of when I was ill for a few days to illustrate their degree of commitment to the course. Instead of taking the time off, the majority of our group still attended the lesson.

As one student said:

> " We'd have felt guilty if we just went home. This has never happened to me on any other course. But we knew that Sharon had prepared the work and I'd have been really fed up if I'd have done all that work and the teacher was away. You just couldn't go home, could you. We actually felt competent to do the work even though you weren't in the room. I've never thought about it before, it just seemed like the natural thing to do like. It wasn't as if we were, um, doing it for the sake of it. It just seemed the thing to do."

This shows that the majority of the group, when presented with learning in this manner, did show a greater degree of commitment even though one student stayed at home.

It would be wrong, however, to imply that the introduction of democratic learning methods was not without problems. One issue which I perceived to be a problem was when two members of our group failed repeatedly to hand an essay in on time. Most members of the group felt that I should have chased these people up much more quickly. But because I felt that this was their course, I was much more lenient than with the Sociology group who had chosen a more traditionally-based course. Finally, after repeated requests, and many comments from those who had completed this task I used my power as a teacher and commented on their profiles. One member of the group felt this was wrong, arguing that although they had moaned repeatedly at these individuals, I did not have the right to use this power if we truly were involved in a democratic learning environment. Perhaps ultimately they should be allowed to fail! I would argue, however, that this was part of their commitment to the course and they could have chosen to leave if they had wished. With hindsight I think this should have been made clear in a contract at the beginning of the course. This illustrates both a professional and educational dilemma. While I would find it very difficult in my present environment to allow a student to fail voluntarily, I actually think that they should have this choice. I personally found this a real dilemma because it represented a contradiction between my own theoretical position and practical application. My idealism tells me what ought to be done and my experience tells me what can be done. Although I found it a frustrating experience to be accused of "selling out" on fundamental principles, I would argue that what I have tried to do is to shape my practice to conform to my principles. To be an educational innovator, as I try to be, is to operate in the world as it is, and not as I would wish it to be. It means facing conflicts and doubts which are difficult to handle. Whether it is right, however, to make compromises and how far to do so, remains a real dilemma for me.

The students saw the issue of power as an interesting one. They felt that we had different types of power. One commented that they had the power to vote with their feet, although he said they did not use it. They also said that they had the power to choose the course and that even though this could have been overridden by my position I had chosen not to use it. They therefore felt that power was used wisely. Another said:

"No, I don't think power was a problem. By setting up a democratic learning environment, power was shared by all members of the group. We chose the type of course and the content of the course. Power is spread evenly around us all."

Many of the above comments refer to a greater group cohesiveness, a greater bonding than might otherwise have occurred. There was a real team spirit, all members of the group commented on how upset they would be if anyone failed. They felt a great responsibility for each other, and the course. This was reflected by the high level of commitment and involvement in the course. They saw both group and personal satisfaction as their ultimate goal, which seems to have stimulated them and made learning more exciting and innovative.

The above comments illustrate that a democratic learning environment can provide many opportunities for group decision making and its component skills. It encourages self reliance in a situation in which students learn to utilise each other's expertise, as well as individuals and groups inside and outside the school. They developed in confidence through continued public speech, in teaching and discussing with each other. It was also a collective experience because of how they planned their course and shared ideas with one another. I therefore regard the democratic learning co-operative as relatively successful.

One way people might measure the success of this venture is by exam passes, which in fact were two points above the national average based on GCSE results. More importantly though, a group of people have learned how to cooperate and help each other, which is a more valuable skill for everyday life. This also illustrates the fact that such group decision making encompasses a number of the other skills of political literacy - constructing sound arguments based on evidence, expressing one's own beliefs and interests through an appropriate medium, participating in political discussion and perceiving and understanding the viewpoints of others. Young people also need to have mastered the necessary political skills to be able to operate successfully in a democratic society. One thing clear from all the literature, is that there is a strong case that these skills need to be developed at school because they do not come naturally. Furthermore, young people need to acquire self-confidence in expressing and justifying opinions, and the only way that these skills will be developed is through experience. Schools therefore need to give young people the chance to participate in decision making in a democratic way!

A second case study

The second group to opt for a democratic learning environment was the 1992/4 Advanced Level Sociology group. Seventeen students opted for the democratic learning co-operative and two opted for the consultative model. Interestingly, no students opted for the traditional method of teacher-directed course or for the Open University type course. They felt that the reason they had chosen the democratic learning co-operative, was because it offered an opportunity to take control over their own learning and because of the possibilities of developing their ideas through discussion.

At the pre-democratic stage the students were given a specimen democratic learning contract. This consisted of a written contract which laid down the ground rules for a democratic learning co-operative (DLC). In fact the previous DLC had suggested the idea. After selecting this method of learning the group decided that it was important to look at writing a contract of their own. The original contract presented to the students was one devised by Harber and Meighan for the PGCE course in Social and Political Education at The University of Birmingham (1986). This process of devising a contract was a long and at times painful one. In fact the contract was changed four times before the group felt it represented their own feelings and requirements.

After completing the contract we proceeded to devise a time-table of areas of study. They had already chosen the areas from the syllabus that they thought would be of interest and now individuals and groups of students went on to select areas for which they wished to be responsible. All students took part in a number of presentations. A box containing work prepared by them and the groups logbook were kept in one of the Sociology rooms to be consulted and used as appropriate. Presentations made use of the full range of teaching and learning styles. In fact the range was far greater than would normally be the case.

The final session of the first term was a review of the course. This was the last session before Christmas and was quite relaxed with the group bringing in the traditional mince pies, etc. Most members of the group had completed a short written evaluation of the group's work and these were circulated before a discussion of the course.

These quotations are taken from some of the students written evaluations of the course and are representative of the group as a whole. They demonstrate their enthusiasm for the course as well as some of their fears.

Effort and responsibility

On a positive note David said:

"Because people know that they have the responsibility of taking lessons they are likely to put a lot of effort into their presentations."

Learning by doing

Sonia said:

"I find myself looking forward to lessons knowing that in some way they all differ. However, I feel that some people are falling into the trap of routine lessons of handouts. I think they should put more effort into the novelty aspect of videos, speakers, role plays, visits etc. It all aids our learning experience and if you are interested you are more likely to remember more."

Interest

Kelly said:

" I think the democratic learning co-operative this term went quite well. Most of the lessons were very interesting."

Yin said:

> "The democratic way of learning has been very interesting and enjoyable. It has been different to all the other lessons in other subjects and has proved that learning can be fun and interesting".

Skills

Julie said:

> "I think having to do the research for the lessons ourselves is a good way to learn the topic, it improves our research skills and you have to understand it better so you can explain it to others".

David said:

> "Pupils contribute more in discussions so grow in confidence when talking in groups. Skills such as these may not be used so much if another form of learning was used".

Success of the democratic learning environment

Most students commented on whether the democratic learning environment should continue. All of the students, except one, said they wished this method of learning to continue.

Yin said:

> "I regard the democratic way of learning as most worthwhile and so I think that we ought to continue with it ... People now know what to do in order to improve upon their first presentation and make it more successful the second time around".

Simon said:

> "When first voted for, I voted against the democratic learning, I am now in two minds, I can't decide. The presentations have been excellent so far."

Sarah said:

"I think we should continue this democratic learning situation as I feel I have benefited more learning this way."

Sonia said:

"We've made a good start on the democratic learning co-operative and have a good foundation to continue with confidence."

Kerry said:

"The course has gone really well, I will be voting to continue with it!"

After the Christmas holiday, disaster struck. I developed a serious illness and was away from work for the rest of the half term. This had a profound effect on the students and eventually led to the downfall of the democratic learning co-operative.

On my return, the students said they felt insecure, and to quote them, 'mucked about'. They asked me to teach the lessons for the next half term which was a five week block. It was agreed that we would continue with group presentations after the Easter holidays and defer the next vote until Whitsun Half Term. With hindsight this was a major mistake, but I was concerned to make them feel secure again and agreed to their request. Before breaking up for Easter I asked the group who would be presenting the sessions after the holiday. They said they wanted a vote on whether the DLC should continue, because they had all discussed it and had decided that they did not want it. I pointed out that this was not what we had agreed at our last meeting and, although I had fulfilled my part of the agreement, they were now going back on a democratic decision.

All hell let loose at this point and normal relations broke down. There was an awful atmosphere in the room and I felt I had no choice but to agree to a vote, with the majority wanting to return to traditional methods of teaching. I explained that this would return all the power to the teacher and that I felt this was not a wise move. Due to their emotional state, however, they did not seem to understand the implications of this decision and insisted that we went down this route. After the vote I decided to make a point. I decided to allocate each student a presentation for the following term. The students were incensed and said they did not want this but I reminded them that they had just voted to allow me to decide how to teach and in my professional judgement I had now decided to teach in this way. Understandably they were furious and felt cheated and completely powerless.

On reflection I should not have allowed the vote to take place because it was undemocratic for two reasons. Firstly, one member of the group, the other member of staff, was not present and we had previously agreed that a vote would take place only if every member of the group had been given the opportunity to attend. Secondly, the students had excluded two members of the group from their discussions, namely myself and the other member of staff.

Later the following day (the last day of term) I was approached by a very concerned Head of Sixth Form. A group of seven students had been to see him and were very upset that I had said we had a democratic learning environment, but that I was not allowing them to have what they wanted. He was in a very difficult situation, because although I had kept the Head of Year 12 informed of the democratic learning environment, the over-all Head of Sixth Form had no idea what was going on.

This was an interesting development because although the students had voted to return to a traditional learning situation, they had been empowered by the skills they had developed through taking part in the DLC. This situation could have created real problems if we did not have the support of other colleagues and highlights the importance of keeping key people informed.

This course of events was basically the end of this particular democratic learning environment. Even though the second democratic learning environment came to an untimely end in the second term, there were still considerable gains. Firstly, a mandate had been gained from the students themselves rather than from external imposition. The act of consultation meant that the students experienced greater motivation. A further gain was that an agenda of possibilities had been set and at least the group had been able to experience an alternative approach for a substantial period of time.

The main strength of the democratic learning experience is that it helped two groups of young people to overcome fears of different kinds, which may prevent them from taking a democratic role in society, such as the fear of speaking in groups, the fear of admitting ignorance, or the fear of expressing an unpopular opinion.

Possibly one of the most important practices of the democratic learning environments was that of dialogue between students and teachers, of questioning and discussing how we might improve our practice. If democracy in the classroom is about anything, it is the free exchange of ideas. Without this open continuous debate, power-sharing is pointless: with it, the place of power in education can be perceived as relating appropriately to teaching and learning.

The experience of the second democratic learning environment indicates the need to encourage the process of democratic practice, rather than assuming that they are already present or arise spontaneously. Unless we are content to be 'represented' by the most articulate in society, we need to give all young people the experience of participating in decision making in a democratic way.

The two democratic learning environments seem to indicate that learners learn best when they are at the centre of the learning process and where they are involved in the doing. You only had to look at the attendance at the sessions to see that the students considered them to be worthwhile.

Moreover, the democratic nature of learning produced greater responsibility and group effort than is demonstrated in the more traditional classroom. As time progressed, there developed both a feeling of considerable camaraderie and a desire not to let everyone down. This manifested itself in several ways. Firstly, meetings occurred between some group members at times and venues outside the usual sessions and the groups thoroughness of research was also far beyond expectations.

Furthermore, the youngsters quality of learning increased. They felt that much of the material had been retained in their long term memories and that they had learned a lot more than in the more formal areas of their educational experience. They also shared the workload, and had a part in planning their own course.

Having experienced successful democratic learning environments I often wonder why others find it so threatening. It is a much more interesting and useful way of working, than I have experienced before. Sometimes I feel it is making an issue out of something quite simple. It is difficult, however, to appreciate that it is a unique approach, until you talk to other groups of students and teachers who employ traditional methods. For many students the transfer of power is long overdue while most teachers seemed horrified at the possibility of relinquishing their captive audience.

In my view, the development of democratic learning environments in schools, with its potential for harnessing the impulse towards co-operation, could be a means of eliminating some of the wasted talent of students, who demonstrate, in their analysis of situations and in their capacity to act on them, quite extraordinary judgement and interpersonal skills.

Conclusion

In concluding, the democratic learning environments offered two groups of students a unique opportunity to experience the processes of democracy rather than the narrow goal-orientated methods of purely didactic education. The democratic learning environment did not merely reflect the world of which it was a part, but it offered a mechanism for coping with a variety of problems. Some values, like those of democracy, tolerance and responsibility, grow only with experience of them.

References

Harber, C., and Meighan, R. (1986) "Democratic Method in Teacher Training for Political Education" in *Teaching Politics* Vol 15, No 2., pp. 178-187.

Meighan. R., "The Democratic School" in *Anatomy of Choice in Education* R. Meighan and P. Toogood (1992), p.103, Ticknall: Education Now.

H.M.I. (1989) *Park Hall School.* D.E.S.

Suggested Further Reading

Harber, C., and Meighan, R. (1989) *The Democratic School* Ticknall: Education Now.

Kohl, H. (1988) *36 Children* Milton Keynes: Open University Press.

Head Teachers and the Challenge of Choosing Democracy

by Paul Ginnis and Bernard Trafford

Head teachers who want to democratise 'their' schools have different reasons for doing so. One might be seeking to improve the school's communication and decision-making procedures. Another might want to motivate students or re-motivate cynical teachers. A third recognises the need to train middle managers in the ways of senior management. Then there are those who want to improve team work, morale or ethos; and those who need the school to better its academic results, truancy figures or disciplinary record. These are just some of the **pragmatic** concerns encountered in the daily life of a school management consultant. In each case the answer is likely to be found in creating some sort of democracy.

Then there are **ideological** reasons. The fundamental right of every human being to be involved in governing her own life is a moving force for some. Others stand in the tradition of humanistic psychology, believing that people want to flourish and will do so only in conditions of high self-esteem and responsibility. The philosophy of the commercial quality gurus (Peters, Ishikawa, Oakland, Handy et. al.) with its emphasis on productivity through people, also convinces certain heads. All of these ideologies, each from a different angle, point in the same direction: towards empowerment.

In the consultant's experience it is rare to find a head teacher who is motivated first and foremost by ideological rather than pragmatic concerns. Bernard Trafford is such a head.

*   *   *   *   *   *   *   *

Bernard Trafford, headteacher of a former boy's grammar school, now a co-educational independent day school, has begun to spread democratic practice. His starting point was a conviction that all the teaching staff needed to be as fully involved as possible in decision-making, but he soon came to realise that there needed to be a fuller commitment to democracy for students too. Such an approach calls for headteachers to have the courage to let go and abandon the traditional assumption of omniscience. The benefits include a shared sense of purpose and an enormously increased motivation among teachers and students alike.

Ten ways in which democracy has been developed in Wolverhampton Grammar School

1. Creation of a Student Council
2. Establishment of a 'right of appeal' or 'right to be fairly treated' for students
3. Promotion of the concept of the importance of students as individuals
4. Promotion of pastoral care as an individualised process
5. Encouragement of close contact with parents
6. Encouragement of students to attend consultation meetings with their parents
7. Promotion of the need for students to learn to take responsibility for their own lives and learning
8. Promotion of the caring aspects of being a teacher
9. Promotion of student-centred approaches to teaching and school organisation
10. Forming alliances with students and teachers against the pressures from outside school (see 'obstacles' below)

Ten of the obstacles encountered

INTERNAL

1. Teachers' fears of criticism from empowered students
2. Students' expectations of teaching as the 'spoon-feeding of knowledge'
3. Fear of taking risks, especially in these days of league-tables and market forces
4. There are contradictions in a head's attempts to impose democracy
5. Democracy takes too much time and effort; for many teachers life is simpler if heads make decisions, leaving them to subvert and complain

EXTERNAL

1. National Curriculum requirements take up nearly all the week and all the energy

2.   National Curriculum requirements limit choice for students:
     empowerment without choices is meaningless
3.   People outside school expect children to be passive and submissive - and
     are offended if they appear otherwise
4.   The 'world outside school' still sees good schools as authoritarian, if
     benign, with 'good discipline' and a rigid uniform code
5.   The 'world outside school' still sees enlightened, good management as
     being related to a traditional authoritarian industrial model.

At a recent seminar Bernard was questioned rigorously about the extent to
which his relinquishing of authority was genuine. Given that he was still held
accountable by his governors, there was a strong suggestion that he had created
a benign and generally acceptable tyranny, not democracy at all. Much
discussion centred also on the Student Council, its scope and power and, again,
the question of whether it really had any clout except by the goodwill of the
head.

These were thorny questions and not easily answered. At the time of the
seminar, Bernard was half-a-term into his fifth year of headship, so the process
may be said to be still in its infancy. He felt that by taking every opportunity to
demonstrate his belief in a democratic style of management he could build
trust. For Bernard, as for all head teachers who tread the democratic path, the
relationship between *authority*, *responsibility* and *accountability* has to be
defined, redefined and redefined again as progress is made.

The importance of the Student Council's reporting back was debated. This
could be done through representatives having formally allocated time with the
forms that elected them; this would need considerable support from the
teaching staff. Alternatively, the Chairman and Secretary could report back to
the whole school during a school assembly. Bernard described how he had
started with a rather more informal approach, disliking constitutions and
formal procedures. His experience, though, and that of many seminar
participants, was that the need for formalised procedures became more
apparent as democracy progressed. Nonetheless, it remains important for
Bernard to change the culture with parents, and in the governance of the
school, by involving teachers and students in as many *informal* policy-making
opportunities as possible.

*   *   *   *   *   *   *   *

It could be said that there are degrees of democracy. Torrington and Weightman's sliding scale (from coercive consent *to* co-operative control) and that of Caldwell and Spinks (from the headteacher alone deciding policy without seeking information *to* headteacher, staff and the community deciding through a formal structure) are just two helpful models. They provide frameworks for plotting progress and planning further democratic developments.

When assessing the degree of democracy in a school there are two key questions to ask:

- **who** is included in the decision-making process - teachers at various levels, students, non-teaching staff, governors, all parents, community representatives?

- **how** are they included in the process - asked for information, asked for opinions, asked to raise issues, asked to set agendas, asked to generate options, asked to decide between options, given autonomy to solve problems and take initiative, given control of resources?

How far does a school have to go along these two continua before it can call itself democratic? Where would Wolverhampton Grammar be placed?

Then there is the question of procedure. For some, democracy is not democracy unless it conforms to some kind of *committee procedure.* Constitutions, formalised representation and voting rules can, however, invite mistrust and conflict, and are open to wheeler-dealing. On the other hand, they do protect rights and guarantee participation. While they are clearly appropriate in some circumstances, they are perhaps a last, rather than a first, resort in schools. Some head teachers fear, rightly perhaps, that traditional democracy of this sort will play into the hands of disaffected staff and students who will use it to take revenge.

Another type of democratic practice is created by those who come at school management from the angle of humanistic psychology, either intuitively or with an explicit awareness of, say, Client-centred Counselling (Rogers), or Gestalt Therapy (Perls), or Transactional Analysis (Berne). With an emphasis on self-esteem, personal responsibility and group support, this kind of democracy is based on the deliberate creation of trust and open communication.

Informal procedures succeed because of the value placed on key interpersonal skills such as active listening and assertiveness, and on key attitudes such as unconditional positive regard and empathy. A minimum number of Ground Rules replaces a written constitution. The resulting modus operandi is flexible. It is able to be spontaneous and creative in a way that formalised democracy is not. However, it only succeeds inasmuch as participants are prepared to live by a code of honesty and mutual trust. Can the varied human natures in any motley collection of teachers or students sustain this high ideal?

By these standards not all democracy is good democracy. Most formalised procedures create losers. They also create laziness; participants do not have to work for consensus - a majority (even a slim one) will do. Then those with this majority can claim a mandate to impose their will on a huge minority. Power seekers, desperate to meet their own emotional need for control and glory, find ways of bullying or tricking, (by witholding information, for example) ordinary souls. Democracy becomes a game, one most suited to the devious and needy and therefore not at all appealing to the average headteacher!

So, it is possible to be disempowered by democracy. Empowerment is an emotional as well as a practical matter. Even when opportunities for participation are offered, few people will take them if they fear being belittled by 'the opposition'; they would rather surrender to the bullies. It is not enough to create democratic structures. Without empowering attitudes and interpersonal skills they will be no more than empty shells.

The empowering process requires people to be listened to, genuinely; it requires all ideas to be valued and integrated one way or another into the pool of communal thinking; it usually requires training in group work skills, both for the chairperson and the participant; it requires a firm intention to achieve consensus first and compromise second - voting comes in a very poor third; it requires the elimination of sarcasm and other forms of put-down. At root it requires a belief that the institution is 'owned' by everyone in it. To start with such a process needs to be led by a head (for in most schools only a head is in a position to lead it) with clear vision and understanding, advanced personal and interpersonal skills, and an abundance of energy. Hands up those who qualify.

Ideologically this is a far cry from the apparent democracy of enlightened industry. Although some of the language and practice is similar, the intention is significantly different: one is person-centred, the other productivity-centred, (and therefore manipulative, it could be said). Likewise, the gut intention, the underlying purpose, of the democratising head teacher will inevitably determine the *type* of democracy to emerge.

So, there are options. Let us define the kind of democracy we want to practice in schools. There is little point in students imitating the pseudo-democracy of our major institutions. Instead, let us prepare them to improve it. The attitudes, skills and structures of humanistic, person-centred democracy can be learned. But beware: *children don't do what they learn, they learn what they do* (John Dewey)!

For further reading:

Trafford, B. (1993) *Sharing Power in Schools: Raising Standards* Ticknall: Education Now Books.

Jones, S. (1992) *The Human Factor: maximising team efficiency through collaborative leadership* London: Kogan Page.

Birmingham City Council (1993) *Quality Development Resource Pack* Birmingham City Council.

Torrington and Weightman (1989) *The Reality of School Management* London: Blackwell.

Caldwell and Spinks,. (1988) *The Self-Managing School* Lewes: Falmer Press.

Brandes, D., and Ginnis, P. (1990) *The Student-Centred School* London: Stanley Thornes.

Minischooling as Democratic Practice

by Philip Toogood

Student participation in learning how to learn

Democracy provides for freedom to take part in self-government. The structures of democracy are designed to enable this self-determination to happen. The device of minischooling in large schools aims to return to the learner that freedom to take part in one's own learning which is so often denied in the standard large school organisation.

Schools generally are more suited to employing teachers than to making the necessary arrangements for students to be able to learn. Schools all too often teach students how to be taught rather than how to learn for themselves. Although it is necessary that a student should become skilled at being "taught" this is not the only, or the main, or the most efficient way of arriving at learning.

Schools, therefore, subject the student to curriculum prescriptions which have been laid down externally to the student. They are authoritarian in this regard and this prevents the autonomy of the student. This does not prevent practically every school from asserting loudly that they teach students to learn how to learn. More often than not, the more assertive the school is in alleging it is teaching how to learn, the more this public display conceals the real situation - that the student is being told what to do, how to do it and how the student is performing according to criteria that the student has had no part in devising.

The factory school model

One main obstacle in the way is often said to be the immense size of the contemporary school. This argument has been used in the past about factories as well. How can you have worker participation in the enormous factories of today?... it is said. Industry, however, has faced up to this one and has largely restructured along the lines of slimming down to "core businesses" which work with satellite companies and are constantly enlarging or contracting the size of the cluster of associated enterprises to suit both the emerging needs and to tap the creativity of the work force more effectively. The large comprehensive school which was created from the time of the 10/65 circular of Harold Wilson was developed because it was thought that the concentration of facilities and expertise on one site would make it possible for the "captains of industry " to be spun off the production lines of the nation's schools more fitted to earn and learn than had been the case with the previous system of schools.

Education has no bottom line

The large size of these schools need not obscure the fact that if these schools were to be restructured following the same organisational principles of con-temporary business, but with due regard being paid to the important fact that a school is fundamentally different from a business, then it would be possible for the freedom to learn how to learn to be accomplished in large schools. This restructuring is simple, easy to do, less costly than to continue on the present tracks, and would introduce the possibility that most of the current problems in large alienating schools could be swiftly overcome. The system of restructuring is known as "minischooling" and it is defined as:

a device for ensuring the effective control by learners over their own learning by returning decisions to the learners and teachers together, within the agreed constraints of being federally part of the wider school.

Restructuring is easy; the territory of the minischool is the learning area, the timetable is decided for the mini- rather than for the macro-school, the team of teachers is personal to the minischool and is not an occasional visitor, the things used are the equipment of the minischool or are withdrawn from a central resource area/library and the planning is undertaken by the team with the students.

What is more difficult is to provide an organisation which will suit the oper-ation of this flotilla of small vessels. Even more important is to make sure that the values of the altered system are present in action in the day-to-day experience of the students and teachers in their altered roles.

No academic/pastoral divide

The old specialist departments have gone, so too have the teams of specialist teachers working alongside each other and supporting each other in their collective identity as "the Science Department", etc. The pastoral hierarchy has gone, along with Heads of Year, pastoral tutors, and Deputy for girls' welfare.

No bolt-on schools councils

There is no longer any need for a whole school Council to spend ages making decisions about social matters in the school (the curriculum, of course, always was a secret garden, guarded by the teachers even if they are no longer the gardeners now that Sanctuary House has usurped the right of determining what should be learnt). But the matrix of constraints, from the learners' agenda to the teachers' agenda still exists. The old mechanisms for resolving conflict (which did not work, so an authoritarian regime had to run) have gone. No longer do herds of students charge round corridors as the lesson bell goes. No longer does a timetable of wondrous complexity rule every moment of the school day set once and for all at the start of the year. No longer is all the technology for this top down factory system stored in the cupboards of specialist departments. No longer do teachers stay behind after school for endless departmental meetings. In fact, the whole arrangement for making decisions about Time, Territory, Teaching Teams, Things and the Thinking processes which plan and review all this, have been returned to the small minischool team and the students.

Honey, we've shrunk the school!

At this point the minischool can become simply a miniature version of what went on before. Indeed in Primary schools there is a considerable culture which proclaims that because just one teacher teaches one class, then all is well. Small is Beautiful rules (except that the class happens to be 35!). This is perhaps the worst of all worlds. Authoritarian schools which are small do not even provide for packaged choice between one brand of authoritarianism and another.

Teacher as reflective agent

The key to the democratic practice in minischools is the altered role of the teacher based on the notion that the minischool is a device for returning decision making to the learner, partnered, supported and advised by the teacher. The teacher acts as a sort of "reflective agent" in the student's learning. This is very similar to the role of a coach in athletics. Only the athlete can do the event and take part in the sport. Only the athlete can determine the degree of participation, the effort, the commitment, the vision, the practice, the sense of partnership with the opposition. The coach, however, is there in support and intervenes across a spectrum of intervention styles from the authoritative to the facilitative, having always in mind an unconditional positive regard for the athlete.

Democratic practice

The good coach will not set targets for the athlete, but will involve the athlete in the considerations which will lead to the undertaking of certain courses of preparation and training. There will be a negotiated (and therefore democratic) agreement on the determination of work to be done. There will be a student-led direction of the search for resources, for the resource of instruction, of investigation, of mid-activity review, of change of direction, of collaborative partcipation with others, of co-learnership with the teacher, of student teaching student, of student teaching teacher, of an exchange of power and a collective review of progress. All this will depend on the teacher being willing and able to carry out this flexible role.

It is very important to distinguish between the reality and the appearance of democratic practice. So often is it the case that the teacher is simply "sugaring the pill" and is gaining skill in imposing external will upon the learner whilst masquerading as a democrat. This is colonising paternalism or maternalism. Minischools where this sort of facade is present quickly become islands of curriculum paranoia. This is more likely to be the case in a system with an imposed National Curriculum, because it will actually be the job of the teacher to gain acceptance by the student for what is being imposed arbitrarily.

Government finds it difficult to accept the real democratic practice of the minischooled large comprehensive when the aims of the government are to destroy local democracy and to harness the young learners to the dictates of one ideology. Thus Countesthorpe, specially built in the 60s to be a minischooled large comprehensive in Leicestershire, Sutton Centre in Sutton in Ashfield, and Madeley Court School, Telford, all flourished for a while but were "nobbled" by inspections which were politically slanted towards an orthodoxy not concerned with democratic practice, except to stamp it out.

Ownership of knowledge

This orthodoxy was based on the absolute validity of the "subject based curriculum", the intellectually disreputable notion that knowledge exists outside the knower in areas or bodies of discrete facts which have to be "known" by learners. This is quite different from the notion that knowledge is largely the creation of the learner either individually or in a social context. Enough was learnt about minischooling by the Madeley Court experience for the largest school in England, Stantonbury Campus in Milton Keynes, to fight to become a Grant Maintained school in order to preserve its comprehensive ideals which, it was felt, could best be preserved and developed in a restructured minischool framework of Halls, or small sub-schools on one campus.

From campus to community minischool

I was Head of Madeley Court for seven years when we conducted this experiment and since leaving have had the good fortune to be able to take the idea of minischooling out into the more radical form of minischools within the community. In 1987 I was invited by parents to keep open the school in the village of Ticknall, South Derbyshire, as an all-ages, independent, non fee paying, parent-teacher-student cooperative. After 7 years, backed by the Education Now publishing, research and consultancy co-operative, we have been able to split off a growing secondary section to the nearby village of Willington (Willington Village College), have a full Primary section in Ticknall (Dame Catherine Harpur's) and have received a glowing report from the recent full Ofsted Inspection.

In this environment we have developed a practice which is relevant to any form of educational project, from Home-based, through Flexi-time agreements, to parent-organised clusters supported by a small centre, to small schools either freestanding or in clusters, to large schools which may be to a greater or lesser extent based on learning areas rather than teaching areas ... in other words "minischooled". This range describes the agenda of the Human Scale Education movement and is actively promoted by the Education Now Midlands-based co-operative in its publications, conferences and consultancy ventures.

Co-operation, self management and democracy

This more flexible education from 4 to 16 years relies on three pillars of support: co-operative management, self-managed learning and democratic decision-making. These have to be jealously guarded against the prophets of "management efficiency" and power bids which masquerade underneath the plausible plea for "financial prudence".

Responsibility for own learning

The whole tenor of the days is a consistent but highly varied pattern from age 4 to 16. Days start with meetings in circles deciding what will be in the sessions and discussing all manner of considerations related to how we live from day to day in this small community with the children. As they get older from the age of 6 years, they assume more and more responsibility for their own learning in 4 different sorts of time, Plan and Review, Independent Studies, Directed Studies and Activities. These often integrate so that Activities becomes channelled into Independent Studies and the planning becomes a part of Activities or Independent Studies.

The Primary section is more recognisably a small school with walls than is the Secondary section. The actual school in the secondary years IS the democratic process operating within the cooperative Tutor Group and developing the learner managed learning. Clearly this Secondary section is not so tried and tested as the Primary and. of course, the secondary stage, being nearer chronologically to the "real world" of adult life is more controversial. There is more of a stark contrast between what we do day by day in the Secondary and the neighbouring vast comprehensive. The subject base and the specialist delivery mechanism of the large comprehensive contrast vividly with the more Open University style of the small Tutor Groups working day by day with the Tutors to develop a pattern of learning which will eventually put the whole management of their education into their own hands.

The Village College, Willington, the Secondary section of the Dame Catherine's School, is effectively a small secondary school, comprising two learning groups of students, one of 11 to 14 year olds and the other of 14 to 16 year olds. It is working a programme called "Flexi College" and is the first of a federation of such "Schools without Walls" (as the first issue of the student magazine was entitled). Flexi College is defined as a flexible college in the community. It is a college not because it is a school, but because of the common contractual basis of membership, between the student and the Tutor, between the Tutor and the student and between all participants and the collectivity of the Tutor Group. It aims to avoid setting learning apart from the community of business, or the family or everyday life, but is set in the middle, supporting and reinforcing the interests of the individual and society in a way that institutions set apart find very difficult to do. The intention is to abolish the duality of education and living. This was also the intention Henry Morris set out in 1925 for the Village Colleges in Cambridgeshire in his famous Memorandum which was arguably the foundation document of Community Education in this country.

The tutor

The two Tutors are Philip Toogood and Richard Terry. Richard Terry writes from his experience of becoming a flexi college tutor about the democratic practice in the school:

> *"As a co-operative learning group we are constantly reviewing, criticising and revising our methods, times and practice. However we do try to maintain a core structure which underpins everything we do, based on the assumption that it is desirable for all students to learn to take responsibility for their own learning. This does not happen overnight, nor with the greatest of ease; on the contrary, it requires hard, often stressful, work. Also required are: a readiness to accept and adapt to changes; and above all the careful nurturing of a set of relationships based on mutual respect and trust."*

Students have an experience of small group living, work experience, community service, vocational   training and academic courses. They can prepare for a wide range of GCSE examinations and for other recognised qualifications. The whole of the Flexi College has grown out of the experience of Dame Catherine's and of the minischools for which I was responsible as Head of Madeley Court Comprehensive in the late 70s and early 80s.

The Flexi College method

Although the Flexi College is a sort of minischool in the community, the actual method of working is applicable in a wide variety of institutional settings. It could be used in the closed world of the Boarding school, in the Private school or in the ordinary local school, Primary or Secondary. What has been invented and is being pioneered is a method of re-inventing school, of re-schooling more appropriately for the times which require young people to grow up to be capable of working co-operatively in their own and in society's interests. The diagram that follows explains how this is so. At the centre is a process of Plan-Do-Review by the individual learner with the Tutor and with the small Tutor Group. Around this is the assumption and development of the three pillars of agreement; co-operation, self-management and democratic practice.   The setting for this life is the Tutor Group, a small intense community where human relations are faced up to and not avoided. The tools that are available for the task of learning are the whole planning process as embodied in the Personal Learning Portfolio and Plan, the available Mentors and the whole Information and Communication technology (every student has a laptop notebook computer in the Flexi College. The curriculum is in clover leaf form of four leaves: Study, Work, Skills and Expressive Arts.

Daily routine

The days are started with half an hour's exercise, incorporating very many different sorts of exercise from Tai Chi to straight forward aerobics. This is followed by a group consideration of the day's news from the early morning Radio 4 recorded broadcast. This is logged and later fed through to a databank to be used in Humanities studies and for later issue as a digest of interest to young and old locally. A short group meeting then takes place for 15 minutes to make the arrangements for the day and to bring up any urgent points for decision. This is followed by a break until 1030.

Supported Independent study assignments are then undertaken individually or in small groups until lunch, 90 minutes later at midday. Both groups then go out by transport to public play areas, sports centre, public library, tennis club etc. A picnic lunch is eaten wherever the student has gone and the afternoon session begins again at 1.30 with a half hour session of writer's workshop, or reader's workshop or numeracy workshop. At 2 p.m the afternoon Activities start (Art, Drama, Design Technology, Humanities or Information Technology). The day ends at 3.45 unless students wish to stay for a further voluntary session. Agreed assignments are continued for homework. During the Independent Studies time on Monday, students have individual tutorials when the assignments are agreed and reviewed. On Fridays between 1015 and 1045 the students' logs are reviewed individually with them and a short Tutor group meeting is held to get ready for the whole school meeting from 1045-1130. Three or four expeditions are planned and held every year and students run most aspects of these themselves, supported by the Tutors. The heart of the whole process is the everyday practice of direct democracy.

Further reading

Meighan, R., and Toogood, P. (1992) *Anatomy of Choice in Education*
      Ticknall: Education Now.

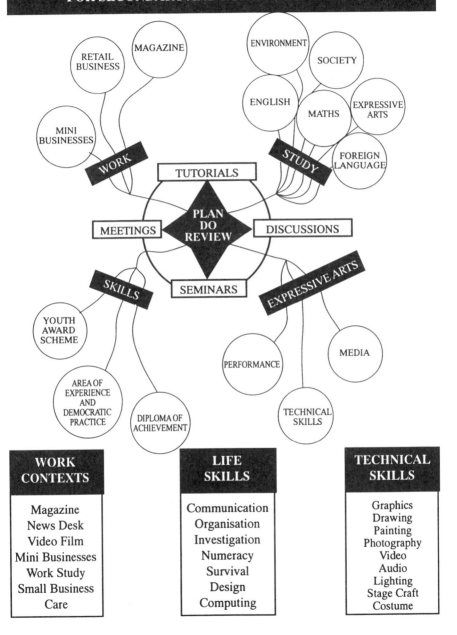

THE FLEXIBLE LEARNING FRAME
FOR SECONDARY AND FURTHER EDUCATION

MAGAZINE

RETAIL BUSINESS

ENVIRONMENT

SOCIETY

MINI BUSINESSES

ENGLISH

MATHS

EXPRESSIVE ARTS

WORK

STUDY

FOREIGN LANGUAGE

TUTORIALS

PLAN DO REVIEW

MEETINGS

DISCUSSIONS

SKILLS

SEMINARS

EXPRESSIVE ARTS

YOUTH AWARD SCHEME

PERFORMANCE

MEDIA

AREA OF EXPERIENCE AND DEMOCRATIC PRACTICE

DIPLOMA OF ACHIEVEMENT

TECHNICAL SKILLS

WORK CONTEXTS	LIFE SKILLS	TECHNICAL SKILLS
Magazine	Communication	Graphics
News Desk	Organisation	Drawing
Video Film	Investigation	Painting
Mini Businesses	Numeracy	Photography
Work Study	Survival	Video
Small Business	Design	Audio
Care	Computing	Lighting
		Stage Craft
		Costume

Learning Democracy Through Drama

by Josh Gifford and Sharon Robinson

Introduction

The theme of "learning democracy through drama" is so rich and varied that a whole conference or book or area of research could be devoted to it. In this article, as in the workshop on which it is based, I will share two activities which I hope will provide examples of how democracy can be approached through drama and provide the basis for further discussion and exploration.

When I was asked to present a workshop on the theme, I was naturally prompted to examine my own practice of teaching drama in a comprehensive school. The main difficulty I found was defining the two terms. The word democracy is open to many interpretations, as is the perception and practice of education through drama. At the risk of being over-simplistic, Drama, in my view, explores what it is to be human, to be alive.

Democracy is concerned with how we attempt to live fulfilled lives in the context of society. Democracy is learnt through drama, because drama, using a wide range of conventions and techniques, explores how it is to be human in the context of society.

For the participants at Bilston College I offered two activities I had shared with two GCSE groups as part of a longer project. I will refer to the two GCSE groups as groups A and B and the Bilston College group as group C. Groups A and B had decided to explore the problems faced by homeless people in our cities. In preparation for this it was decided to create a large scale map of a British city. Each member of the group was given a large square of art paper on which to draw a section of the map. At the end, all the pieces were to be sellotaped together to form a completed map. This out of role activity would create the basis for our exploration through drama. The task would require skills of negotiation, cooperation, imagination and the ability to create a shared world.

Group A, a large group of twenty-four, decided that discussion and negotiation would be needed before drawing took place. They felt that this was particularly important at the borders of each square. It was comparatively easy for participants to map out their own areas but negotiation was vital at the borders, particularly for those with squares in the middle of the map. "Will you extend my canal?" "Will you complete my shopping centre?" Decisions were also made about what kind of area each person would map out and what colours and symbols would be used. The group decided it would be easier to split into three groups of eight, each complete a third of the map and then join all three together. The students worked in a relaxed and purposeful manner, those who finished first helped others and there was regular discussion and negotiation throughout the task. "We need a mosque." "Can you help Peter, he's getting behind?" "We need a homeless shelter somewhere."

At the end of the session, the three sections of eight squares were sellotaped together to form a detailed map full of possibilities for exploration. Follow-up discussion revealed a high degree of enjoyment with the process and satisfaction with the map produced with an acknowledgement of areas which could have been approached differently.

Group B, a group of eighteen, encountered problems with this task. Some members of the group realised that discussion and negotiation were needed, but many quickly set to work developing their own areas without considering or purposely avoiding the practical problems or interpersonal issues presented by the task. These participants had their heads down, focused on their own section of the city, only occasionally looking at others' work. The atmosphere was purposeful but there was tension developing between those attempting to develop an overall strategy and those mainly concerned with their own area. The inevitable problems arose when these participants had to negotiate at the borders - their inner space was so full of their own creations that they had little space to accommodate anyone else's! "I can't extend your motorway, there's no room." "I'm not having your lake near my zoo." These border skirmishes brought frustration and some entrenched positions. Although the finished map represented the random way most cities have evolved, and therefore presented possibilities for subsequent work, the process had been far less pleasant for the participants in group B. Follow-up discussion, however, revealed an awareness of the problems the process had presented and from this we developed some more appropriate approaches to group tasks.

The mapping exercise shows how through a seemingly simple task, we gain insights and understandings about ourselves, about others and about group process. I feel it is unnecessarily restricting to consider that drama takes place when participants are in role, inside the drama. For me the drama starts when we walk through the door into the drama space.

Group C, the Bilston group, approached the tasks in a similar spirit and manner to group A, although they had less time to complete the task.

For the second activity we decided to make the city more "real" for ourselves by looking at how differently people perceived and experienced the city. The G.C.S.E. groups had time to do this from a number of perspectives but in the short time available for the Bliston workshop each participant was asked to be in the role of a police officer responsible for the area of the city they had created. I was in the role of the newly appointed chief constable for the city who had convened a meeting to gain information about the policing policy, issues and problems of each area of the city.

In general the G.C.S.E. groups highlighted the problems of vandalism, violence, drugs and a general fear of city life. In contrast the Bilston group was particularly concerned about the underfunding of the police force, the emergence of vigilante groups in areas where policing was considered inadequate or ineffective and conditions of service and low morale. Members of this group were keen to impress on me that they were looking for prompt action to address these problems.

We were now deepening and expanding our understanding of the city we had created, and it was becoming more "real" to us. At this point a decision has to be made: where do we go next? I call this the "crossroads" area of the process.

At the start of the project the G.C.S.E. groups stated that they wanted me to make the most of the directional decisions at the "crossroads" leaving them to influence the direction of the work through out-of-role activity e.g. the map, and in role activity, e.g. the police exercise. The belief in the city we had gained provided a sound basis for our work on the problems experienced by homeless-people and we developed a number of dramas using several techniques and conventions which members of the group felt expanded their awareness in this area.

If members of the Bilston group were to have influence over directional decisions at the "crossroads" some of the possible options would be:

1) Developing beliefs in the city; developing empathy.
Would you like to explore the way the city is perceived and experienced by other groups of people: taxi drivers, people living on the Croxley estate, shopkeepers?

2) Developing ideas identified by the group.
From the issues you have identified as police officers, I can suggest the following ways of exploration:

(a) a group of residents meet to discuss the formation of a vigilante group follow-ing a number of burglaries and violent attacks in the Hillside area of the city;

(b) a series of tableaux (frozen pictures) showing the range of crimes committed in the city on Saturday, followed by thought tracking of the participants and onlookers;

(c) the new chief constable is visited by members of different sections of the community who express their concerns about crime in the city.

3) Offering a wider brief
Do you have an idea on this theme you would like to develop in small groups or with whole groups?

Clearly a great deal more space could be devoted to the complex and subtle area of negotiation of work in drama and this exercise merely points out some of the possibilities. I feel one of my main aims as a drama educator is increasingly to share power with members of the group. Members of drama groups shape and influence the drama process through what happens both in and out of role. Their work as participants, discussing and negotiating in an out of role task, participating in role inside the drama or discussing and reflecting on work in or out of role maintains a constant dynamic with the facilitator of the work. The two activities I shared at conference indicate how democracy can be approached through drama, how we can learn about ourselves and our relationship to others through participation in group processes. The work in role shows how drama can evolve from the interests and concerns of the group and through a process of discussion and negotiation at the "crossroads" of each process.

The map-making illustrates the challenge we face as individuals in society, the challenge of remaining uniquely individual but matching our inner map to the map of the world. Paradoxically, the more successful we are in reaching out to others, the more fulfilled we feel inside. It is no coincidence that members of group A, who showed as much care for the group as they did for themselves, seemed relaxed and at home in company and content when working alone. They seemed to have it both ways, and so can we. In this context aiming for a truly "rich" democracy has implications for our inner health in contrast to a spurious "rich" democracy for the minority of this country engineered by years of institutionalised selfishness. As Stephanie Downick writes in her book "Intimacy and Solitude,":

> "Dante spoke warmly of an "intellectual life filled with love." This beautiful phrase describes to me a life in which thinking (about people, about how we live, about life's meaning for ourselves and other people) is honoured, but also suffused with love which leads the connection to spontaneity of feelings and from there to action if that should be appropriate."

In conclusion, I feel that drama presents us with potent and practical ways of achieving the inner qualities required to explore the attainment of a "rich" democracy.

....

Sharon Robinson writes: from Josh's description and analysis of just one starting point for dramatic action, it is easy to see the rich potential for learning through drama.

If there were a more widespread belief in democracy, we would probably see a natural rebalancing of the arts and sciences in our educational thinking. It seems logical to me that human beings should naturally seek knowledge and understanding about how their emotional, spiritual, social, as well as their physical world functions.

Not all drama teaching is democratic but Josh's teaching is a clear illustration of democratic practice.

First, the lesson structure is democratic. This is easy to see. The active technique used to stimulate thinking creates accessibility for many learning styles and levels of ability. The result is a shared understanding and vision, creating an equal basis from which to build the next stage of the lesson. The starting point is sufficiently open for members of the group to use their own ideas and to identify their own areas of interest.

The teacher than asks the group how they would like to be involved in the development of the drama and gives them genuine options. The group has the opportunity to be creative and is given security through positive interactions with the teacher who is clearly in a supporting mode.

Second, the structure of the lesson is underpinned by the **teacher's relationship with the group.** The teacher's declared intention is to share power with the group and to achieve this he must work from the principle that learning best occurs in an environment characterised by mutual respect. This requires the teacher to develop and maintain a genuine and truthful relationship with the learners. He must also hold the belief that all people are responsible for their lives and are capable of making significant decisions about their learning.

The way the group responds to the options that are offered depends on its members' levels of skill and their understanding of, and interest in, the material they are working on. The teacher must make judgments about the most useful strategy to employ to support the learners. This might mean at one time giving them a strong challenge or at another suggesting an activity. Sometimes the teacher will recognise that the students need more time to talk before they are ready to find their own path as a group. As long as the relationship between the teacher and the learners is based on listening, a real process of discussion and negotiation can take place.

To summarise: democratic practice is about the teacher's desire and ability to share power through the thoughtful creation of participatory **structures** and through the teacher's **interpersonal skills** which facilitate the management of learning **with** the learners.

Drama offers significant learning about self and society. It is a dynamic model of reality through which we actively as participants, or passively as audience, experience the world. Learning through drama is unique because it is learning which is FELT. Drama conducted in a democratic manner is most likely to achieve this **engagement of feeling** because it automatically locks into the participants' own thoughts, insights, confusions and desires. Only when drama achieves this engagement, and consequently achieves **learning through feeling** for the participants, has it operated as a true art form.

References

Brandes, D. and Ginnis, P. (1986) *A Guide to Student-Centred Learning,* London: Stanley Thornes.

Thornes Dowrick, S. (1991) *Intimacy and Solitude*, Australia: William Heinemann.

Morgan, N. and Saxton, J. (1987) *Teaching Drama: A Mind of Many Wonders* London: Stanley Thornes.

Community Arts - Cultural Democracy

by Kate Gant and Mark Webster

Introduction

Kate Gant and Mark Webster are Community Arts Development Workers with Walsall Community Arts Team. Together they explore the values behind Community Arts and pose the question, is it a democratic practice?

We are all bombarded with images and ideas created by other people. The Community Arts movement developed as a response to the closed doors of elitist art and the increasing saturation by and commercialisation of popular culture. Community Arts offers people a voice and a representation in the development of culture. Control over people's own cultural identities strengthens the ability of individuals and groups to participate equitably in the local community and the democratic process.

Community Arts activity takes on a set of values which underpins the practice whatever the art form. This definition defines the arts by purpose rather than type. It makes no distinction between art forms. The underpinning values are just as relevant in the visual, performing and media arts.

The values that underpin Community Arts work

Every group that seeks to develop Community Arts activity is different but the values which underpin the work of Walsall Community Arts team are broadly those that underpin the movement as a whole.

- **Local people**
  Community Arts work happens in communities with people who share a sense of identity or a sense of purpose. Therefore, the single most important principle behind arts and cultural work is that local people are consulted with and listened to and that their needs, aspirations and culture are reflected and developed through the work.

- **Access**
  People are methodically excluded from the arts at an early age and are encouraged either to believe they have no ability or that the arts are not important to their lives. This process is underpinned by the mechanisms which create social and economic disadvantage. Community Arts prioritises work with groups who are otherwise excluded from arts to ensure that barriers to participation are broken down.

- **Participation**
  Community Arts is not done to people. Projects and activities involve people as planners, creators and audiences.

- **Empowerment**
  Community Arts activities have to enable people to move from a position of dependency or inaction to a point of effective self confidence. Not only in relation to the arts activity but in organising future activities with others.

- **Partnership**
  Community Arts recognises that change and development happens through collaboration. On a practical level this means partnership with and between groups with many diverse interests and cultures but with a commitment to the same core values.

- **Quality**
  As with all democratic work there is a tension between quality of process and quality product. In the past the Community Arts movement has been criticised for valuing process over product. There is now general agreement that work that does not value quality in both process and product is counter productive.

The arts encourage people to communicate and seek creative solutions. It is a process which links the imagination to the production of products or events which say something relevant both for the artists and the potential audience. When art is created democratically in groups by people with a common issue, interest or culture it is a powerful tool for individual growth, group empowerment and social change.

Most democratic work will prioritise some or all of these core values. The arts are simply another ingredient which effectively combines with **all** the core values to give people tools to change their lives and give voice to key issues.

Of course everybody does creative things everyday. Singing, dress making, making plays, writing poetry, cooking. Community Arts workers seek to value and foster these and other activities to enable people to use them collectively to give voice to issues which need shouting about and to celebrate their own cultures.

Community Arts methods work effectively in schools; however, like most democratic activity they engenders change, both in perceptions and power relationships. The approach encourages people to share common experiences as well as recognise differences. So within some voluntary communities or authoritarian institutions like schools, Community Arts methods lead to a questioning of authority and a challenge to the existing power relationships.

Community Arts methods work effectively with groups on housing estates, in community halls, youth clubs and temples simply because people have chosen to come together around an issue, activity or common cultural experience which binds them together. The arts in this context is a very powerful tool for change.

The role of the Community Arts worker

The Community Arts worker has a number of roles and in fact, like any activity, there is a number of processes happening at any one time. A good example of the work of the Community Arts team in Walsall is the work done in partnership with people on the Beechdale Estate.

Beechdale is considered a problem estate in Walsall where, so the popular myth runs, nothing ever happens. Nestling under the motorway it does face a lot of the multiple social and economic disadvantages common to urban areas.

In 1990 the Community Arts workers from the team started talking to people on the Beechdale about what they did and what they would like to do. The result was a banners project which involved over 60 local people from 10 different groups in making banners which profiled themselves and shouted about the positive things they would like to see happen.

People were enthusiastic and wanted to continue to be involved in more arts projects. At this point a crucial decision was made. A core group of local people agreed to form an independent group - Beechdale Arts Forum. This meant that local people, with support from local community workers and Walsall Community Arts team, could plan and deliver their own year-round programme of activities to meet the needs of people living on the estate.

In the last year they have undertaken a large-scale community play, an annual arts festival and carnival, a lantern procession, a variety show and are currently starting rehearsals for a pantomime. All this would not have been possible without the work of many skilled arts practitioners who have been employed to enable people to develop the skills necessary to plan and undertake projects. Some of the best textile artists in the country, dance animateurs, theatre directors, writers, musicians and all manner of makers have worked with local people so that they can value skills and gain new ones.

And the Financial Cost? In a time of limited resources how can it happen? Instead of the Arts being seen as a luxury, Walsall Community Arts Team argue that the arts are an essential tool for non-arts agencies to achieve their own goals. Hence, funding partnerships have been made with a number of urban regeneration agencies as well as traditional funders of arts activities.

Obviously the development has not been straight forward and the role of the Community Arts workers from the team has itself developed. Broadly speaking we have moved from being an initiating body to an enabling body. In other words, we now work with people on their projects on the Beechdale instead of asking them to help out on ours.

By offering Management support, access to training in project administration, advocacy with funding bodies, and just straight forward advice, we now put together a project by project contract for services (rarely money) to enable them to achieve their own plans.

Every project and every group we work with is unique. Our work on the Beechdale is not a blue-print for work elsewhere. It does, however, illustrate the way in which it is possible to put the core values into practice. Our long term aim is to create an infrastructure of services and local resources to support this kind of activity while at the same time continuing to help create new opportunities and new areas of work.

Conclusion - is this a democratic way of working?

Yes! A lot has been written and said about cultural democratic practice or cultural democracy. Common to all debates is change. Change in people's attitudes, roles, power relationships, change in our expectations of who participates in arts activities and as a result of being involved in a creative process, producing a quality end product. Change as a result of people working together.

Within the Walsall context Community Arts Development officers offer skills and resources to enable changes to occur. We believe if these are offered in an open accessible and fun way within the spirit of dialogue, partnership and co-operation the sky is the limit.

Further reading

Barnham, Lynne (1994) *Starting Out:An information pack for artists and arts organisations* Coventry: Coventry City Council.

GLC (1986) *Campaign for a popular Culture:A record of struggle and achievement achievement: The GLC's Community Arts Programme 1981 - 1986.* London: GLC.

Kelly, Owen (1994) *Community, Art and the State* London:Comedia.

Matarasso, Francois. (1994) *Regular Marvels;A handbook for animateurs* London: C.D.M.F.

Walsall Community (1992) *Dreaming for Real: Planning the arts in your Community* Walsall: Walsall M.B.C.

Willis, Paul (1990) *Moving Culture: an enquiry into the cultural activities of young people* London: Calouste Gulbenkian Foundation.

Democracy and Equality of Opportunity

by Anna Frankel

Introduction

Does a democracy require equality of educational opportunity? Is it possible for democratic values to subsist alongside educational inequality which may either be planned or, according to socially agreed measures, be judged to achieve unequal outcomes? Can apparently democratic institutions operate within societies where there is widely different access to employment of material, political and cultural benefits? In fact, is there a necessary link between the two concepts: democracy and equality of opportunity?

Democracy and Equality

One obvious way to answer the questions is to conduct an exploration of the various meanings which adhere to the two terms 'democracy' and 'equality of opportunity'. Not surprisingly, given the long histories of the concepts of equality and democracy, they have been frequently reinterpreted in order to meet particular ideological circumstances; there is no single definition which can be usefully produced. Nevertheless, demonstrating the range of interpretations does begin to provide some answers to the questions posed in the first paragraph.

Democracy was understood by the ancient Greeks to be rule by the people. But, as is well known, the most powerful definition of people was free man. This definition played a major part in shaping the particular demands to increase democracy, which have been and continue to be made up to the present day. Historical record shows a development from pressure for one free man, one vote through to one competent adult, one vote. This model of democracy may be described as the right to political representation.

Other equally powerful enactments of democracy have been via the traditions established during the American revolution. Effectively, this has meant democracy has been understood to be the defence of liberty which, in practice, has meant various enactments designed to ensure freedom of choice.

Democracy, in this context, is not about the right to be represented by individuals of the population's choice but about individuals having the right to create their own lives. In some cases, this emphasis on choice has led to individuals apparently choosing to live in pitiful conditions because the majority of the population does not choose to make provision for the community as a whole. Effectively, this second understanding of democracy is about individualism; the defence of the right of the individual to make choices which may be detrimental to others.

It is possible to see that these two major understandings which have dominated Western culture and political ideology for centuries are, in many respects, contradictory. MacPherson has demonstrated that pyramidal representation, commonly found in capitalism, is continually compromised. The need to mediate between social groups extremely unequally placed with regard to material and social goods makes open lines of up and down responsibility impossible to maintain.

The word 'equality' has had an equally tortured history. A major consideration in conceptions of equality has been the comparator. To argue for equality inevitably means making claims for equality with another group; after all, you cannot be equal with yourself. What has always been contentious is gaining the agreement of the comparator that they will so act. Racial equality was contentious in the French revolution when the claims of black Haitians to be included in the drive for equality were variously accepted and rejected by the white elite during the French revolution and its aftermath. An immediate precursor of the civil war in America was the question of equality. Can a modern capitalist society include an economy based on slavery? As the answer was clearly 'no', a major barrier to the development of the individualistic democracy or market based capitalist economy which we recognise today in the United States was swept away.

The second problem regarding comparison is the relative merits of comparing individuals in contrast to comparing social groups. Comparison between individuals has been treated as a means of justifying both the maintenance of huge inequalities and demands for greater equality. The argument that no two individuals are alike can make both minor and major differences acceptable. Group comparison depends upon constructing a group and, particularly in these post-modernist times, traditional social groups are immensely fragmented. Post war claims for equality made by and for black people are now more likely to be articulated as claims for equality by black women, Asians and other ethnic interests.

Questions of equality and democracy are drawn together when the issue of action regarding the promotion of equality is considered. Effectively, adherents of radical individualism argue strongly against any organised promotion of equality on the grounds that interference in the rights of individual choice is more damaging to the social fabric than any potential improvement in equality. The view here is that individuals are equal and will, therefore, find their own level.   In other words, promotion of equality is not needed when equality already exists.

Other views regarding promotion of equality lie nearer to the opposite end of this particular continuum in that action of some kind is favoured. At various stages, the barriers have been identified as lack of political representation, lack of education, legalised differences in pay and so on. Much effort has been put into obtaining extensions of laws and reinterpretation of rules in order to achieve equality. Other sets of arguments regarding barriers have focused on the cultural and ideological sphere, where the debate has been about theories of difference. At times, apparently critical differences have been found, between for example men and women, and yet a century later, the original thesis may have been either entirely rejected or reinterpreted beyond recognition.

Democracy, whether interpreted as individual choice or representation of collective political interest, does not require equality between individuals or groups.   Inequality can be suffered or welcomed as a measure of the effectiveness of a democracy. Even when active intervention takes place, such actions may not be highly valued by the majority of the population, irrespective of the particular position within the social hierarchy.

Notwithstanding the absence of a necessary link between democracy and equality, it is still reasonable to ask whether democracies might benefit from equality of educational opportunity. Treating educational inequality as a sub-category of inequality, it might be possible, or even desirable, to establish some standard of equality within the educational field which does, in fact, uphold the democratic principles of the particular society. It is to this debate which we now turn.

Education

Education is the process whereby individuals acquire intellectual and emotional independence. The means whereby this is or should be achieved has exercised the thinking of practitioners and theorists alike in every known society.

A considerable literature is devoted to the importance of preserving and/or promoting individual choice in education. Maintaining this interpretation of democracy requires as much social engineering as the more traditional understanding of positive action typically associated with schemes designed to enhance/achieve educational equality. Defending or promoting choice appears to involve investing the country's resources in individual educational units, either apparently or actually outside state control. Whether such investment is carried out by the state on behalf of individuals or by individuals themselves, usually affects the degree to which individuals really are choosing the type of education they want for themselves or their children.

Other preferences for equality as individual choice tend to focus on the concept of the democratic classroom, or the teacher as facilitator of the individual's learning programme. Taken as they stand, these approaches are even more desocialised than the choice model for they can and do disregard the question of whether the individual chose to participate in that learning programme. Democracy within institutions that few chose to attend has a slightly absurd feel about it. In contrast, an expensive private school might be able to operate this model more effectively.

Choice, it is argued, benefits democracy and is not to be confused with selection. Choice can be exercised by everyone whereas selection is exercised by a group on behalf of others. Examples of selection in education include the old tripartite system and election of dons at Oxbridge colleges. Both systems have been criticised for their lack of, if not opposition to democracy and also for their failure to produce enhanced equality of opportunity and/or outcome. Determining the veracity of such claims depends upon which groups are compared and what particular interpretation is placed upon equality.

If the word education is understood to mean what is learned as opposed to how learning takes place, then there is an immense history of curriculum studies devoted to establishing exactly what education for democracy might mean.

Dewey devoted considerable energy earlier this century in arguing for instruction in the social scientific method to be made available so that people would learn how to promote their interests through the democratic process. Marx and European Marxists did not bemoan the absence of political education but urged the study of philosophy whilst emphasising the need for workers' organisations themselves to educate their members. Latterly, doubt has been expressed about the capacity of the education system to provide any kind of education for the majority of the population. Feminists and black radicals often denounce state education. There is a distinction to be drawn between education for the masses, with its connotations of equality and education for democracy. Mass education, which is a hallmark of contemporary capitalism, sits uneasily with the notion of democracy as freedom of choice even if it fits adequately with its antithesis, representative democracy.

What about attempts to use the education service to close the gap between various groups? Some treat cultural difference as the key issue. But how effective have those policies been which have treated inequality as a major barrier to democracy? Such educational projects range between those which are a response to violently expressed demands or a moral panic about the conduct of the materially deprived, to those which provide training for the power brokers. Between these two extremes have been and continue to be a range of initiatives which, whilst usually couched in term of vocational aims, frequently target resources at groups which are materially deprived.

The short sharp shock recently attempted by the prison service with its absence of comprehensive education and training was an attempt to create citizens able to participate in a capitalist democracy. In contrast, race equality training for institutional managers is designed to ensure that they do not discriminate and, in some cases, actively reduce inequality in their sphere of control. Between these extremes are the heavily funded European projects which combine employment, vocational training and social need criteria. Again, although the project criteria do not explicitly mention democracy, the social need criteria suggest concern amongst these ideologues regarding the political risks of supporting a large, relatively uneducated, poor.

All of these projects probably do improve the life chances of some individuals who pass through them or whose manager passes through them, so in that sense they contribute to reducing inequality. They may well, too, encourage individuals to exercise choice and participate in representative democracy.

Conversely, they often reflect a diminution of choice for the very groups who experience most inequality; those who can exercise choice, do not choose the youth training scheme.

Conclusion

In answer to our questions. Democracy (whatever its form) does not require equality of opportunity or equality of educational opportunity but is probably assisted by collectively agreed measures which, as it were, interfere with the democratic process. Institutions with varying degrees of democracy can cohabit within an unequal society. But, there is a distinct danger that, to paraphrase Peter Tosh, everyone is crying out for democracy, none is crying out for justice, but there will be no democracy, till people get equal rights and justice.

References

Abercrombie, N, Hill, S and Turner, B S (1984), *Dictionary of Sociology*, London,   Penguin Books.

Arato, A and Gebhardt E, Eds (1978), *The Essential Frankfurt School Reader*, Oxford, Basil Blackwell.

Held, D et al Eds (1983), *States and Societies*, Oxford, Martin Robertson and Open University.

MacPherson, C B (1977), *The Life and Times of Liberal Democracy*, Oxford, Oxford University Press.

Oakley, A (1981), *Subject Women*, London, Fontana.

Stuart Maclure, J (1965), *Educational Documents. England and Wales. 1816-1963*, London, Chapman and Hall.

Tosh, P (1984), *Equal Rights/Downpressor Man.*

Tuttle, L (1986), *Encyclopedia of Feminism*, London, Longman.

International indicators of democratic schools

by Lynn Davies

Introduction

The notion of 'performance indicators' is increasingly used in education, as in other public sector institutions.   For schools, this has traditionally meant indicators such as examination achievement, and indeed the major focus for the 'effective schools' research has been the cross-national or between-school comparisons of performance   either on specially designed tests or in public examinations.   More recently, 'equal opportunities' in countries such as UK and USA has also been translated into sets of indicators, so that schools and colleges can evaluate progress on ethnic or gender equity, how far the school is using unbiased materials, or how far staffing and authority structures are a true representation of the mix of gender, race, disability, sexuality or age divisions within the school community.   Democracy, however, has not been subject to such audits. The 1994 OECD collection *Making Education Count: Developing and Using International Indicators* pays scant attention to anything social or political, and concentrates mainly on cognitive attainment. This is in spite of arguments raised in international arenas for human rights, such as the Council of Europe report *Socialisation of School Children and their Education for Democratic Values and Human Rights,* where it is argued "There is an immediate need to develop performance indicators for school climate" (Starkey, 1989).

Other contributors to this volume will be arguing for the benefits of democratic practice itself in schools; one of the few significant quotations in the OECD collection was from a 1988 study on school climate by Evans and Hopkins, which suggested that: *"the more open and democratic the school climate and the more self-actualising the members of the teaching staff, the more effective their use of educational ideas in practice".*   Here, democracy is being conceived as a useful tool for something else;   I would argue that it is a significant goal for schooling in its own right.

If it is such a goal, then I would argue further that it can profitably be subject to translation into indicators within educational institutions.   At first sight, democracy may seem too amorphous or diverse a concept to be broken down into tick lists, especially for use internationally. Such an endeavour seems also to be acceding to the current market-oriented drive towards customer accountability and the reduction of all life to Standards Institute measurement. However, crystallising what democracy might mean in practice is important for a number of reasons.

Firstly, the very fact that the word carries so many meanings and interpretations means that it is essential to attempt to identify what it signifies in daily routines of educational life. When the term 'democratic' can be used in the title of, for example, a large range of political parties in various parts of the world, some of which appear more repressive than participative, it becomes clear that the word can become meaningless unless attached to certain sets of conditions and conditionalities. 'Western democracy' can be equally viewed with suspicion by developing countries, or by countries with different religious bases, who see it as code for permissive, subversive or sacrilegious in intent. Because the ideal of democracy carries within it, by definition, the seeds of flexibility and openness, it becomes equally open to use and abuse as a label. Translating democracy into visible and agreed signs is one way to avoid mistrust or complacency.

Secondly, and developing the above argument, the very exercise of trying to arrive at indicators of democracy is a very useful way of exposing core values in an institution. Staff and student discussion and debate around what could be seen to be democratic practice is almost more important than the eventual checking of reality against the ideal.

Thirdly, having in place a set of indicators for democracy in a school is an essential balance to the otherwise increasing obsession with examination results and league tables of academic achievement. Unless the ways schools are organised for future political orientation is given equal prominence and publicity to their competitive and selective function, they will continue to serve narrow interests. A particular head may be able to democratise a school, but if that personality leaves before such democratic practice becomes codified, then powerful interests may well persuade a school back into the focus on the measurable. Using the management-speak of 'performance' may smack of 'if you can't beat them, join them', but achieving a set of democratic indicators is more than just playing the measurement game. It is an essential display of a school's commitment to a set of values and purposes which can be central to large scale issues of human rights and world peace. No amount of examination qualifications and certificates will protect you from the Scud missile or the tribal incursion.

Definitions of 'indicator'

We should perhaps clarify what is meant by an 'indicator' before proceeding further. It is taken here as *an item of information relating to school practice which reveals the extent to which wider goals are being addressed and met.* It is a sign, a symbol, an operationalising of values. An indicator can therefore be a concrete manifestation (e.g. the presence of a Student Council); a measurement (the number of questions asked by students in class); or a question (how are teachers appointed or promoted?). The main aim is to turn a broad concept such as democracy into smaller items which can be used to assess a school's 'progress' over time along certain dimensions.

The UK Overseas Development Administration for example has four dimensions of 'good governance': legitimacy, accountability, human rights/rule of law and administrative competency (British Council 1993). How can an observer spot these at 100 metres in a school? Even if we break down 'legitimacy' into areas such as participation, consent, the presence of civil institutions or multi-party decision-making, these would still need translating into everyday school life.

A particular interest is whether there can be internationally agreed indicators. Would a democratic school be internationally recognisable? Would indicators that are useful in the UK context be applicable in conditions of extreme stringency, or traditions of one-party rule, or with different intersections between religion and government? The definition of democracy or good government at national level may well determine what a democratic school is deemed to look like in that country. We need to be able to surface and compare the concrete manifestations of adherence (or otherwise) to a political philosophy. An indicator can therefore be a dimension with positive and negative ends along which a school or country can be evaluated - whether on the degree to which freedom of expression is permitted or the degree to which people are informed about the way authority works.

Ways to achieve indicators

Because an indicator is a sign of something deeper, or more hidden, or more diffuse, then there are many ways to arrive at a list. One is for a school or college or group of teachers/students to brainstorm what surface features a truly democratic school (or even a truly authoritarian school) would have, and from the suggestions try to sort them into categories which started to reflect wider goals. A second way is the reverse of this, to start with the goals of the school which relate to democracy and see how each translates into everyday practice. A third way is to look at various areas of school life and work, and ask questions or put quantitative measures on them relating to democratic philosophies. Fourthly, one can take national or official categories such as the ODA ones mentioned earlier, or the UN Convention on the Rights of the Child and attempt to operationalise them at the school level.   It is possible that similar indicators will turn up whatever the procedure, and the initial choice may depend on how far a school or college has already got a commitment to, and an agreed definition of democracy.

Let us take some of these routes to see what commonalities do arise. Firstly, a brainstorming session at the Bilston Community College/Education Now conference in UK produced an initially arbitrary list of what a democratic school looked like. The items ranged from 'political education' to 'smiles', from 'non-authoritarian relationships' to 'the condition of the toilets'. Afterwards, it seemed that these reactions could be grouped in five overlapping areas, as follows:

- **Human Rights:** absence of caning -   absence of bullying - equal opportunities (access to curriculum, staffing etc.) - ownership of space - non-custodial;

- **Participation:** Number of people involved in tasks/ranges of activity - community representation on school bodies - staff/student representation in decision-making - pupil participation: dinners, opinions, administration of the school, setting the agenda, research on democracy - negotiable curriculum - participation in deciding the indicators of assessment;

- **Information**: Levels of communication - compulsory contemporary social/political analysis/political education - varied assessment/evaluation;

- **Mutually responsible relationships:** non-authoritarian relationships - counselling - mutually agreed assessment procedures;

- **School climate or culture:** Smiles - peaceful - number of rules - having no bells -territories - condition of toilets - safe space.

There are similar features here to a list I had previously compiled, attempting to quantify the areas so that some systematic records could be kept to assess progress (Davies 1994):

Structure:
- presence of a School Council
- number of (a) elected positions, and (b) rotating positions in the school
- presence of system of grievance procedures
- presence of student newspaper or bulletin;

Decision-making:
- number of decisions taken by School Council actually implemented
- number of people involved in major decisions
- proportion of rules decided by the students
- instances of group decision-making;

Practice in democracy:-
- number of questions raised by students during a lesson
- number of people using grievance procedures
- instances of pupils choosing to work co-operatively
- instances of open negotiation and compromise over running of school
- presence of real or mock elections or referenda;

Autonomy and taking responsibility:
- number of students voluntarily using library or resource centre
- number of students suggesting work to be done
- number of students and staff organising extra-curricular activities
- community work, community change;

Preparation for active citizenship:
- staff knowledge of contemporary political scene, structure and leaders
- students' knowledge of above
- student confidence and ability to express opinions
- number of students articulating their concerns.

Lest this sound too mechanistic or fanciful, Fletcher (1989) outlined a number of key features associated with schools that have actually operated democratically, putting these under the headings of the people concerned. Under **pupils** were found for example student councils and elected representatives, under **teachers** were staff meetings where they could determine the agenda, and participation in staff selection, under **headteacher** came the emphasis on principles rather than details, and commitment to full circulation of all information, under **parents** came right of open access, and under **governing bodies** was found a balance of interests so that no one group held an effective majority.

Conversely, at a 1994 international British Council seminar on 'good government' in education, an 'indicators' group arrived at ten areas of concern within a school or college, but phrased the points as questions, with 35 altogether. Many are covered by the above examples, but there are some significant additions, such as:

Constitution: is there a written constitution or charter which sets out the rights and obligations of members?

Organisational structure: How were the head and teachers appointed, and under what criteria?

Curriculum: Is community work/action included to give knowledge of the workings of local politics?

Staff development: Are there open mechanisms for promotion and professional development?

Forums for discussion: Who can ask questions of the school? Who initiates a forum for discussion?

The group report noted, however, that it was not able to proceed to the more long-term indicators which would assess outcomes; that is, whether the products of a school were in their future lives acting in ways associated with good government. Translating from broad political dimensions to educational contexts perhaps starts to give the clues to the connections. By using a combination of the ODA definitions (1993), and the UN Convention on the Rights of the Child (1990), I arrived at the following possible translations:

POLITICAL AREA	QUESTION FOR A SCHOOL/COLLEGE
1. **Legitimacy:** Government power	Were those in positions of authority (staff or students) elected with a universal franchise and secret ballot? Can they be removed by a peaceful democratic process?
Political opposition and media coverage	Are there formal channels for opposition to power and decision-making, and ways for that opposition to be communicated and disseminated?
Representation	Do those in a position of authority represent a cross-section of the school and outside community, or are groups systematically excluded?
2. **Accountability** Definition of responsibilities	Are responsibilities (i.e. separation of powers) between different parts of the organisational structure of a school clearly defined and applied?
Audit systems	Are there effective internal and external audit and inspection procedures?
Levels of corruption	Are there high levels of corruption and favouritism in the school? Do mechanisms exist to combat them?
Information	Is knowledge of democracy, rights and political alternatives provided through a political education curriculum? Is information on the activities of senior management available to all participants?
3. **Competency** Political skills	Does the management have the skills and information base to make sound school policies and implement them?
Policy content	Is the school policy and development plan appropriate to the needs of its members?
Defence expenditure	Are resources wisely allocated and balanced?

4. Human Rights	
Bill of Rights	Is there a school constitution or Bill of Rights for staff and students? Is the school aware of the UN Charter of Human Rights, or the UN Convention on the Rights of the Child?
Arbitrary authority	Are all individuals and groups free from arbitrary power and treatment? Is there protection of privacy?
Freedoms	Is there freedom of thought, conscience, religion, movement and association? Is there discrimination on the grounds of gender, ethnic origin etc.? Are minorities protected from oppression? Has the child or teacher a right to express an opinion and to have that opinion taken into account in any matter affecting them? Has the child or teacher the right to obtain and make known information, and to express their views unless those would violate the rights of others?
Legal system	Do the school rules operate fairly, quickly and with open access?
Law enforcement	Are those enforcing the rules impartial and are the punishments appropriate? What are the conditions like in places of detention? Is there evidence of abuse , neglect, violence or humiliation? Does school discipline reflect the child's human dignity?
Private sector economic activity	Is there a framework for independent and autonomous choices of learning or school activities by pupils?

After the list

It still remains to establish, however, what happens with such indicators, measures and questions once agreed and collected. As said earlier, the rationale is that it is important to keep up the profile of democracy in a number of arenas - in whole school development, in educational research, in government policy. The draft for this paper was written while I was in the Yemen, working with the University to establish an M.Ed. degree. The areas for study which had previously been suggested were very traditional ones within psychology, educational administration and Islamic studies. Although this was only six months after a civil war, and fighting was still going on the Saudi-Arabian border, they thought my suggestion that education for peace, or democracy, or tolerance should be included, was quite a novel idea. Anything that smacked of politics was at that time, of course, highly contentious.

It would be good, therefore, to make democracy respectable - boring even. Sets of trialled indicators, automatically part of institutional evaluation, could be used not only for an individual institution to assess its progress, but to keep in the forefront the goal of the school as the production of the democratic citizen. Just as a curriculum subject is not high status unless it is examinable, a school goal is not taken seriously unless it is measurable. It is time to lose our fear of treating democracy with hallowed respect, as a wonderful but essentially intangible philosophy. If to attain peaceful national and international governance we have to translate democracy into the ring-binder manual, so be it. I suspect that unless we are able to make transparent in an accessible way the everyday workings of educational institutions, then we will never be able to make schools contribute to anything except individualism and aggression.

The benefits of 'the list' are that one can start in a small way to take risks with a few of the areas. Democracy is not an either/or state; it is a process, a set of dynamic principles by which groups or institutions try to work towards a sustainable and just way of organising. As Tschoumy said:

> *"Human rights...never gives us a chance to relax....Democracy goes hand in hand with the permanent right to comparison, information and vigilance" (1989 p127)*

It is just such 'comparison, information and vigilance' which could be valuably attained through generating, monitoring and acting on performance indicators of democracy.

References

British Council (1993) *Good Government Development Priorities: Guidelines* Manchester, The British Council.

Davies, L (1994) *Beyond Authoritarian School Management: The Challenge for Transparency* Ticknall: Education Now.

Fletcher, C (1989) 'Democratization on Trial' in K.Jensen and S.Walker (eds) *Towards Democratic Schooling: European Experiences* Milton Keynes:Open University Press.

OECD (1994) *Making Education Count: Developing and Using International Indicators,*

Starkey, H (ed) (1989) *Socialisation of School Children and Their Education for Democratic Values and Human Rights* Council of Europe/Swets and Zeitlinger.

United Nations Centre for Human Rights/UNICEF (1990) *Convention on the Rights of the Child: Briefing Kit* Geneva, UN Centre for Human Rights/UNICEF.

Contributors

Clive Harber is Professor of Education at the University of Natal

Derry Hannam is a former deputy head of a Derbyshire Comprehensive School and an OFSTED Inspector of Schools

Frank Reeves is Vice-principal of Bilston Community College, Wolverhampton

Janet Meighan is co-director of Education Now and Honorary Lecturer at the University of Derby

Roland Meighan is co-director of Education Now and Special Professor of Education, University of Nottingham

Patrick Ainley is an educational writer and part-time university lecturer

Lesley Browne is Head of Social Science in a Birmingham Comprehensive School

Paul Ginnis is co-director of Education Now and a Consultant and Trainer in student-centred learning and collaborative management

Bernard Trafford is Head of Wolverhampton Grammar School

Philip Toogood is co-director of Education Now and Head of Dame Catherine's School and Willington Flexi College

Josh Gifford is a teacher of Drama in a Lancashire Comprehensive School

Sharon Robinson is co-director of Education Now and a teacher-consultant for Drama with Birmingham L.E.A.

Kate Gant is a Community Arts Worker in Walsall

Mark Webster is a Community Arts Worker in Walsall

Anna Frankel is a lecturer at Bilston Community College, Wolverhampton

Lynn Davies is Director of the International Unit, University of Birmingham School of Education

BOOKS BY EDUCATION NOW

Beyond Authoritarian School Management by Lynn Davies £10-00
...vital reading for anyone keen to move beyond the limitations of authoritarian school management into more effective forms of practice

Never Too Late by John Holt £10-00
I applaud this book heartily ... Sir Yehudi Menuhin

Anatomy of Choice in Education Roland Meighan & Philip Toogood £10-00
...precisely what is needed to clear up present confusion and set coherent, purposeful, productive patterns for the future... Dr. James Hemming

Learning From Home-based Education edited by Roland Meighan £5-00
...the rich diversity of the home-based phenomenon is demonstrated.

Issues in Green Education by Damian Randle £5-00
... it certainly succeeds in provoking thought ... Chris Hartnett

Sharing Power in Schools: Raising Standards by Bernard Trafford £5-00
... our students are becoming more effective, self-confident and imaginative learners and workers. Examination results are improving ...

Early Childhood Education: The Way Forward
edited by Philip Gammage and Janet Meighan £7-50
This is essential reading for all involved in the education of young children.

Skills for Self-managed learning by Mike Roberts £5-00
This book reports on a ten year research study into this topic

Praxis Makes Perfect: Critical Educational Research for Social Justice
by Iram Siraj-Blatchford £6-95
The author is a black feminist who has long been concerned with the question of whose knowledge and intellectual frames are represented by the academy.

John Holt: Personalised Education and the Reconstruction of Schooling
by Roland Meighan £9-50
A review of John Holt's contribution to education ten years after his death.

Education Now, 113 Arundel Drive, Bramcote Hills, Nottingham NG9 3FQ

Education Now

EDUCATION NOW thinks that the word *education* has come to be misunderstood. Many people assume that it means 'what teachers do with children in school' and nothing else. **EDUCATION NOW** challenges that view. Its understanding of education is much wider, encompassing the many beneficial experiences which take place outside schools and colleges and which lead to valuable learning. It opposes the elements in the present system which promote uniformity, dependency, and often, a lasting sense of failure.

The vision of **EDUCATION NOW** includes:
- a focus on the uniqueness of individuals, of their learning experiences and of their many and varied learning styles
- support of education in human scale settings including home-based education, small schools, mini-schools, and schools-within-schools, flexischooling and flexi-colleges
- recognition that learners themselves have the ability to make both rational and intuitive choices about their education
- advocacy of co-operative and democratic organisation of places of learning
- belief in the need to share national resources so that everyone has a real choice in education
- acceptance of Einstein's proposal that *imagination is more important than knowledge* in our modern and constantly changing world
- adoption of the Universal Declaration of Human Rights in general and the European Convention for the Protection of Human Rights and Fundamental Freedoms in particular.

EDUCATION NOW maintains that people learn best:
- when they are self-motivated
- when they take responsibility for their own lives and learning
- when they feel comfortable in their surroundings
- when teachers and learners value, trust, respect and listen to each other
- when education is seen as a life-long process

EDUCATION NOW is a forum in which people with differing, diverse and undogmatic views can develop dialogue about alternatives to existing dominant and compulsory forms of education.

Office: 113 Arundel Drive, Bramcote Hills, Nottingham NG9 3FQ

Praxis Makes Perfect:
Critical Educational Research for Social Justice

A division between theory and practice has come to dominate education. This division stretches all the way from the classroom, where teachers 'deliver' a national curriculum, to the university research seminar room, where the delivery often uncritically involves postivistic or interpretative methodological choices.

This book is concerned with educational research and is therefore written for those critical post-graduate research students and researchers who have completed research methods courses, but who have yet to take on the challenge and responsibility of justifying their knowledge claims rigorously.

Iram Siraj-Blatchford writes:
"In writing this book I am aware that many other researchers, students and professionals, who are motivated by the desire to facilitate change with a similar apparent contradiction between their commitment to producing objective, value free research and their commitment to equality and justice. ... I will ague that as 'committed' researchers, we need to move beyond such false contradictions while at the same time accepting a dual role, of empowerment and critical engagement."

"My primary audience is those colleagues who are committed to anti-racist and anti-sexist research. I hope, however, that I have succeeded, to some degree, in my attempts to draw out of the arguments identified, a number of issues of wider significance to all of those engaged, or considering engaging in other radical research contexts."

This book fills a significant gap in the literature on research methods and their implications for social justice.

Iram Siraj-Blatchford is Senior Lecturer at the University of London Institute of Education

ISBN   1-871526-18-3   Price   £6-95

Education Now Books
113 Arundel Drive Bramcote Hills Nottingham, NG9 3FQ